In The Year 2021....

It won't be due to the most depraved, cc .... .istory

In the year 2021

If God's a coming, He oughta make it by then

Maybe He'll look around Himself and say
Guess it's time for the judgment day

You Tory Cunts have had your say
Now is time for Independence Day

In the year 2021
Scotland's Independence will be won
There will be freedom from Tory rule for everyone....

Created by Tommy King using original images by www.wefail.art

If you are offended by bad language or don't understand that I can use the same phrase........
"get tae fuck ya cunt" as a term of endearment and also an expression of anger then stop reading now..

I'll start with a short introduction to myself. I have never written or published any book but last year I started work on my own autobiography as a personal project.

I grew up in a small mining village, Gorebridge, outside Edinburgh. My Politics would be described as Left Wing and I have despised Tory governments and Thatcher with a passion all my life. I am now a very staunch Scottish National Party supporter. But what does Left Wing or Right Wing really mean?

To me it's simple – Left Wing equates to desiring a fairer caring society for all – Right Wing equates to desiring to make the rich richer and the poor poorer. Don't get me wrong I have been in the "Champagne Socialist" category through my own hard work and efforts on several occasions, but I have also been in the gutter more times than a Leith hookers knickers.

I am 63 years old and have been self employed since I was 27 when I was forced to leave a relatively senior management role in the National Coal Board due to my stance on the '84 miners strike and very vocal criticism of the NCB, the Tory Government and of course Thatcher.

www.wefail.art

My career has involved various positions in survey, financial services and renewable energy. This includes reaching Partner status at J. Rothschild, the Investment and Pension firm founded by Lord Jacob Rothschild and Sir Mark Weinberg and my recent experience is designing large scale solar pv systems. This included designing The Solar Pyramid which is on the original site of Bilston Glen Colliery, Loanhead where I worked 38 years prior.

Becoming Partner at Rothschild with Sir Mark Weinberg and the Solar Pyramid Project

https://www.srtenergy.uk/video

After a couple of difficult years financially in commercial solar and under pressure from my daughter and son, Kaleigh and Josh to take a break, I agreed in August 2019. To keep busy I started writing my autobiography which had been in my head for years but was prompted by a chance meeting with Irvine Welsh last year.

After my son Josh saw Trainspotting for the first time, he was adamant that the blonde, fitness fanatic, pool player Tommy in the book/movie was based on myself due to similarities with scenes in the movie with tales I had told him about myself and his granddad Jack Curran, who owned The Tommy Younger Bar in Leith and I lived above it. Also, I was actually a blonde, fitness fanatic, pool player at the time. It transpires that it was a local for the unknown Irvine Welsh who was starting to write Trainspotting . I happened to walk into a pub in Leith last year and standing drinking with a friend of mine, Colin Simpson, was Irvine Welsh celebrating that Hibs had just beaten Hearts. Colin introduced us and I obviously told him the urban myth. He laughed and said he was not going to say yes or no...but I could tell Josh it was definitely true. When Irvine was leaving he came back across to where I was sending Josh a selfie, shook my hand and said "Tommy, we are leaving to go to the Central Bar....I'd be delighted if you would come along and spend the rest of the day with us". The Central was absolutely packed with Hibs supporters who were all keen to greet Irvine and we were constantly interrupted but we chatted enough for him to urge me to write my autobiography, "Diary of A Lucky Bastard" which will be published soon. Is Tommy in Trainspotting fact or fiction? I've never made further contact with Irvine so I can only leave it to your imagination.....but he did say YES.

Tommy **(Kevin McKidd)**

Tommy and Angie

Tommy and Irvine

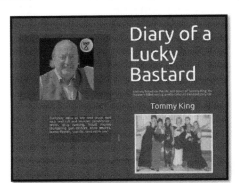

Part of my "retirement" plan was to rent a villa in Spain over the winter months. To fund my trips to Spain I started work as a chauffeur and Aug 2019 – Dec 2019 were simply the most enjoyable months I had for years. I made a few trips to Spain to view villas and in January 2020 decided to set up my own chauffeur business "Spirit of Scotland Tours". I ordered a Mercedes from a dealer in Manchester and was due to collect before I went another trip to Spain.

Chauffeuring at Gleneagles.

In Dec 2019 the outbreak of a virus in Wuhan, China had started to make the news and by mid January 2020 it was clear that this virus may spread to Europe and the UK. I started to question whether the virus could start affecting incoming flights to the UK. I called the dealer in Manchester and explained I would pick up the Merc when I returned from Spain. By the time I came back I decided to delay collecting the car for another few weeks. By March the UK was in full lockdown including wiping out the majority of flights and the tourism business. I had come within a whisper of having a villa in Spain, a new Merc at the front door and in full UK lockdown. Lucky Bastard.

At the start of 2020 Covid-19 lockdown myself and 7 golfing buddies started a group What's App that was a huge amount of fun as despite being very close friends the abuse we give each other is unbelievable....but very funny to our sense of humour. "Lockdown Diary" which is 250 pages of our WhatsApp with jokes, memes and videos has just been published https://www.amazon.co.uk/dp/B08L9PF57P . Lockdown Diary gave the idea of doing something similar by using my own social media posts from the start of the covid-19 crisis.

I am writing this in December 2020 with large parts of Scotland and England in Tier 3 & Tier 4 lockdown, however, the UK has started to roll out a coronavirus vaccine. Biden has been declared the next US President although the moronic arsehole Trump is refusing to accept the verdict and claiming electoral fraud without a shred of evidence.

The following is a diary of social and political personal views of how the Tory's have handled the crisis compared to the Scottish Government, using almost daily fb posts, adult humour, memes and MSM downloads.

The Four Arseholes of the Apocalypse

Created by Tommy King using original images by www.wefail.art

07/01/20. I've had a bit of a fb political sabbatical since the utterly sickening General Election. Although the result will almost certainly give Scotland Independence for which I'm delighted ....I'm sick to my stomach that any individual with any self respect or a shred of compassion could vote for a lying, cheating Tory cunt.

This and establishment electoral fraud are the reason we have Trump, Johnson and Brexit triumphing over sane, caring, compassionate morality ......and FB has played a huge part in this fraud.

So as we head for more deaths of soldiers and innocent civilians remember if you voted for Trump's stooge you have their blood on your hands....because a Tory government is already responsible for the deaths of thousands of vulnerable UK citizens.....so do you think they will care about the deaths of American, Iranian and more UK citizens?

Oh and Happy New Year. Love and Peace Tommy Meldrew.

07/01/20. Scottish referendum vote-rigging claims spark calls for recount

There is irrefutable evidence that the British establishment rigged the 2014 Scottish Referendum, the Brexit Referendum and the 2019 UK Election.....mainly by electoral fraud and postal ballot rigging but also by paying £millions to Cambridge Analytica who were also paid £100,000,000 to engineer the election of Trump. 👀👀

Are you a mushroom who wants' to be kept in the dark and fed establishment shit...or Are you YES yet? "We tend to take the view that if someone knows what the contents of a secret ballot box is before it is opened, then he/she has been involved in, or with, criminal conduct i.e. Rooth The Mooth admitting live on TV that illegal sampling was carried out by Tory's at Indy 1.

https://www.theguardian.com/politics/2014/sep/22/scottish-referendum-vote-rigging-claims-recount-petitions

Others refer to footage that they claim shows a counting officer in Edinburgh writing on a ballot paper.

Maybe I should add "there _was_ irrefutable evidence before fb deleted the video"

07/01/20 . Fresh Cambridge Analytica leak 'shows global manipulation is out of control'

Indy Ref 1, Trump elected, 2016 Brexit vote, 2019 UK GE.......do you want to be a mushroom.....kept in the dark and fed shit....or start thinking and analyzing for yourself? Will you be fooled again at Indy 2? Are You Yes Yet? Make the Indy 2 Referendum beyond the establishment fraud by sheer numbers of YES votes and vote for a fairer caring society.

https://www.theguardian.com/uk-news/2020/jan/04/cambridge-analytica-data-leak-global-election-manipulation

Facebook's Mark Zuckerberg testifies to Congress after it was reported 87 million Facebook users had information harvested by Cambridge Analytica.

11/01/20 FB Memory from 2 years ago

Mhairi Black "We do not fear referendums. We do not fear democracy. We do not fear holding up our vision and hopes for a better Scotland to the electorate to at least consider."

https://www.facebook.com/theSNP/videos/370997477034416

13/01/20. Edinburgh set to cut social care budget despite crisis.

Yeah....cut care to the elderly, shut children's playgrounds, shut public toilets...leave potholes on mains roads so deep a Chilean miner would be scared to go in......but hey let's dig up Leith Walk continuously for 10 years....and spend another £500,000,000 on an unwanted tram system. Has Adam McVey done the decent thing yet? No not topped himself.....just resigned.

https://www.edinburghnews.scotsman.com/health/edinburgh-set-cut-social-care-budget-despite-crisis-1361769

14/01/20. Boris Johnson's Brexit plans will place a no-deal exit firmly back on the table

If you voted for this lying, cheating Tory cunt...you will reap what you sow and your children, your grandchildren and future generations will despise your memory.......but only if they hoped to live in a fairer caring society......if they think like you and are selfish uncaring I'm all right Jack just keep your hands off My Stack Toly's .....I pray you and they get what they deserve. . Luv n Peace. 🍺🍺🍺🍺🍺🍺✖✖✖✖✖✖

https://inews.co.uk/news/brexit/brexit-deal-latest-boris-johnson-no-deal-exit-eu-talks-375836

14/01/20. First Minister responds to Boris Johnson's Section 30 rejection

Democracy will prevail over Tory establishment lies and propaganda. ✖✖✖✖✖✖✖✖✖✖✖✖✖

https://www.thenational.scot/news/18158825.first-minister-responds-boris-johnsons-section-30-rejection/

14/01/20. The Lying, Cheating cunt that is Boris Johnson has suffered twelve defeats in the House of Commons as he continually tried to get his flawed Brexshit deal passed but bleats about respecting democracy? NOWHERE in The Edinburgh Agreement is the phrase "once in a generation vote" stated. In 2019 The people of Scotland overwhelming voted for an SNP manifesto on the basis of 'material change in the circumstances that prevailed in 2014' meant a second referendum was democratically necessary and the precedent has already been set by the British Government that a state has the right to declare Independence without the agreement or permission of the original state and its political or legal authorities".,

I am absolutely staggered that this man has been unable to negotiate a hugely complex trade agreement.

If you wish to be viewed as Statesman like with credibility dress as such.........if you wish to viewed as a Moronic Clown dress as such.

16/01/20. Over Xmas lunch with my very good friends ....most of whom are very successful businessmen but a couple are Unionists..I asked these questions:-

Q 1) Do you consider yourself intelligent successful businessmen? A. YES.

Q 2) OK you are all Directors and shareholders in UK Ltd. I'm the sole Director of Scotland Ltd which is a wholly owned subsidiary of UK Ltd. You continually tell me Scotland Ltd is losing money and needs to be subsidized by UK Ltd? A. YES

Q 3) OK if you are correct that is unfair on UK Ltd and I would like to make Scotland Ltd an Independent company that is no longer a supposed drain on finances of UK Ltd. Is that OK? A. NO

Q 4) OK so you want to retain a loss making company that is a drain on your finances. Do you still consider yourself intelligent successful businessmen?

A. Still fucking waiting....... 🤐 ARE YOU YES YET? ❌❌❌❌❌❌❌❌❌❌❌❌❌❌

25/01/20. The corrupt establishment lies and propaganda in the UK is VILE. 🤬🤬🤬🤬🤬🤬
The only chance we have of creating a fairer caring society is Independence and and voting YES in such overwhelming numbers that even the LYING TOLY KUNTS cannot deny the people of Scotland their democratic rights ❌❌❌❌❌

29/01/20. Scotland to reach 100% renewables in time to host 2020 climate summit

Fucking unbelievable....hosted in Glasgow and the Lying Cheating cunt that is Johnson banned the elected First Minister of Scotland from attending 🟢🟢🟢🟢 Are You Yes Yet......or a submissive slave to making the Rich Richer and the Poor Poorer? ✖✖✖✖✖✖✖✖

https://reneweconomy.com.au/scotland-to-reach-100-renewables-in-time-to-host-2020-climate-summit-60854/?fbclid=IwAR1VPcliLXQWYEOOgbmL_dzh215I6trV6zp7Evw7UtcQp8o_es9IbQrUMqo

29/01/20. OK so watching the "Celebrations" of dragging Scotland out of the EU against the democratic will of a Sovereign Nation......on the John Logie Baird TV, ..singing "for Auld Lang Syne"....toasting with Scotch whisky.....with ice from the refrigerator that was designed Scottish professor William Cullen.........or maybe a G & T thanks to Scottish doctor George Cleghorn. .....spreading the news on the Graham Alexander Bell phone....leaving on the Kirkpatrick Macmillan. A blacksmith from Dumfriesshire, who conjured up the pedal bicycle with Dunlop tyres .....heading for a game of golf...as Scotland is praised time and time again for inventing golf,....then relaxing with a game of Grand Theft Auto the brainchild of Scottish video game design extraordinaire David Jones..... all funded by Scottish oil.........before shagging a "Nell Gwyn" who died from a strain of syphilis....the only thing England invented. ✉

30/01/20. St Nicola ...HONEST, eloquent, caring and passionate about Scotland.

Johnson....LYING, stammering, vile.....and hates Scotland .."The Scotch – what a verminous race!"; "It's time Hadrian's Wall was refortified, to pen them in a ghetto on the other side"; "The nation deserves not merely isolation, but comprehensive extermination". Words he printed. So why is Johnson determined to block Independence? Because he knows an Independent Scotland would become a fairer caring ...and wealthy Nation......leaving England as a divisive, elitist ....and poorer Nation. ARE YOU YES YET ✖✖✖✖✖✖✖ ,

29/01/20. Farage, who's party represents the UK in Europe has just stood up in the EU Parliament with the rest of his Brexit Party MEPs, waved British flags, spewing divisive and hateful rhetoric, cheering on his pals in the right wing Tory party. How embarrassing for the people of the UK, that upon leaving the EU, the UK's representatives in Europe were advised to leave the parliament by the Irish speaker and to take their flags with them, and had their microphones cut off for playground behavior, and rather than leave gracefully, engaged in vile hate speech upon their departure. With a result fraudulently bought by his bum chum Aaron Banks this lowlife piece of shit criticizes "Scotch Nationalism" as decisive 🟢Are You Yes Yet? 🟢✖✖✖✖✖✖

31/01/20. Don't hold your breath....no Doctors or Nurses available to resuscitate you

05/02/20. Alex Salmon, and big SNP fish, was on a trip up North canvassing for SNP. He spent the night in the pub and was making his way back to the hotel when he noticed this beautiful young girl at the side of the road in a wheelchair. He said "Hi are you ok?" she said "yes but would you do me a big favour please?" He said "yes of course...what is it?" she said "would you mind pushing me back to my cottage? It's just the other side of the woods" "Of course " He said and they headed off into the woods. It was a lovely moonlit night and when they reached a clearing in the woods she asked Alex to stop. "would you do me another very big favour please?" she said. "Of course I will...what is it?" "Will you dance with?" me she said. "But you are in a wheelchair?" .Alex said....."yes, but I'll sing and you just spin me round and round" ......She started singing Flower of Scotland and Alex swung her round and round with her short mini kilt blowing in the evening breeze......"that was fantastic.....would you do me one last favour please?" ....."Of course...what is it?" said Alex....."will you make love to me?"......"But you are in a wheelchair?" Alex said......"Yes but there is a big nail in that tree behind us and if you lift me up you can hook the belt on my kilt on the nail and make love to me" .....Alex thought long and hard but finally lifted her from her chair and hung her on the nail and made love to her. "Thank you so much" she said and they headed for her cottage. As they approached up the path the front door swung open and there stood a huge bearded Scotsman ......"Did you just wheel my daughter back home through the woods?" he growled......Alex gulped and said "Yes I did Sir" ......"well thank you and please come in for a Dram" .....Alex nervously went inside and they sat and shared a bottle of Scotch. "Ah can't thank you enough Alex you are a true caring passionate Scotsman..... .that Cunt Boris Johnson jist left her hinging on the nail"......😀😀😀😀😀😀.

07/02/20. France paralysed by biggest national strike in years — Nationwide strike across France.

Why is this not on the BBC News? Why doesn't The Bullshit Broadcasting Corruption want to publicize the working class rebelling against the Establishment but they make millionaire Philip "I buy any Boy dot com" Schofield lead story? Obvious isn't it? Simplze...they are shit scared we might take a lead from the French and stand up for our democratic rights......and let's see what happens when the Lying Cheating Kunt Johnson tries to stop Indy 2".

08/02/20. Kevin Bridges How's your self esteem?

https://www.youtube.com/watch?v=8dwU2jGimkU

11/02/20. David Hencke investigates whyBoris Johnsons Government handed out £1.7 million for election management services without a competitive tender.

Lies, deception, fraud and £Billions wasted ....that's YOUR Government. 🌀🌀🌀🌀🌀🌀🌀🌀
ARE YOU YES YET? 🔷🔷🔷🔷🔷🔷🔷🔷

https://bylinetimes.com/2020/01/07/why-did-cabinet-office-rush-through-procurement-of-controversial-electoral-services-company-idox-just-before-the-general-election/

13/02/20. Boris Johnson's dad receives multi-million pound payout over HS2

FFS....I'm sure the cheating lying cunt wasn't influenced when he gave it the go ahead?
NEWS 25th May 2015
£3.64bn ... how much Scotland may pay for a HS2 line that won't go beyond the Border. What's the figure now? £8bn?

ARE YOU YES YET? 🔷🔷🔷🔷🔷

Janey Godley - Masks

https://www.youtube.com/watch?v=PexdOvu_emA

13/02/20. Sajid Javid, Rishi Sunak, Alok Sharma, Priti Patel, Suella Braverman, Sadiq Khan, Shahid Malik, Baroness Warsi, Lord Desai, Baroness Uddin , Lord Alli, Lord Bilimoria, Lord Dholakia, and Lord Gadhia.....where was this cabinet built? Not Ikea I think.

Maybe these Brexit arseholes had a point....do we need to control immigration? Are they coming over here and taking Englansdshire jobs?

Or are they simply more intelligent, better educated and more suited for responsible positions than the Englandshire Eton Bullingdon Twats?

Ali G for UK PM!!!!

14/02/20. Enjoyed a beautiful Valentines meal for two today.....I've always been a greedy bastard......

16/02/20. **Half of the new cabinet attended Oxford or Cambridge.**

https://www.independent.co.uk/voices/boris-johnson-reshuffle-private-school-oxbridge-a9336461.html

Half of the new cabinet attended Oxford or Cambridge....do you seriously think these £multi millionaires with parasitic inherited wealth are capable of making policies that benefit the majority of a working class nation? Of course not ....they are inbred with the "make the rich richer and make the poor poorer" mentality.

17/02/20. St Nicola ...HONEST, eloquent, caring and passionate about Scotland. 💕✖✖✖✖✖

Johnson....LYING, stammering, vile.....and hates Scotland .."The Scotch – what a verminous race!"; "It's time Hadrian's Wall was refortified, to pen them in a ghetto on the other side"; "The nation deserves not merely isolation, but comprehensive extermination". Words he printed. 😡😡😡😡😡😡😡😡.

18/02/20. So why is Johnson determined to block Independence? Because he knows an Independent Scotland would become a fairer caring ...and wealthy Nation......leaving England as a decisive, elitist ....and poorer Nation. ⬛⬛⬛⬛⬛⬛⬛⬛⬛⬛⬛⬛⬛⬛⬛⬛⬛ ,

18/02/20. I'd definitely bring back hanging......but only for Toly MP's that fiddle with children and expenses....

22/02/20. I watched a really scary supernatural movie on my own last night....don't know what the fuck possessed me

22/02/20. The Postal Ballot at the Scottish Independence Referendum

There is irrefutable evidence that the British establishment rigged the 2014 Scottish Referendum, the Brexit Referendum and the 2019 UK Election.....mainly by electoral fraud and postal ballot rigging but also by paying £millions to Cambridge Analytica who were also paid £100,000,000 to engineer the election of Trump. 😠😠😠😠

"We tend to take the view that if someone knows what the contents of a secret ballot box is before it is opened, then he/she has been involved in, or with, criminal conduct"

Are you a mushroom who wants' to be kept in the dark and fed establishment shit...or Are you YES yet?

https://docs.google.com/document/d/13OPs4c91U4ggD1XrHWGAig8YOoXbehVSEpGwaJJWtpc/pub?fbclid=IwAR364sGBM16j
sfunex9r4e_faDF60DHnyB0cvhTsYoOJq1do7lcUDVnSRe4

25/02/20. House of Lords expenses spiral out of control.

Austerity ....people dying and committing suicide because of benefits cuts......and these £millionaire cunts are paid £30,000 for turning up and sleeping 😴😴😴😴😴😴😴😴😴😴

https://www.thetimes.co.uk/article/house-of-lords-expenses-spiral-out-of-control-36w0cbq5s

11/02/20. Coronavirus: Health minister Nadine Dorries tests positive

Mad Cow Disease would have been more appropriate.

11/02/20. Edinburgh Airport boss blasted for 'profiteering' over £5 pick-up charges

https://www.edinburghnews.scotsman.com/news/politics/council/edinburgh-airport-boss-blasted-profiteering-over-ps5-pick-charges-2442631

Why are the Evening News and Taxis focusing on the £5.00 pick up charge when there are more blatant and horrendous pick up charges for chauffeur hire cars? The charge fee is a minimum £5.00 but this can easily rise to £9.00, £16.00, £25.00. Chauffeur cars even if they wait until a flight has landed get charged from the moment they take a ticket at the barrier but can then be circling inside the pickup zone trying to find a parking space before going to greet their passengers...who may well be delayed by inadequate baggage handling resulting in up to another hour delay which the chauffeur is being charged for. Considering the chauffeur will make multiple pickups in a shift it means each car will be charged upward of £100.00 per day in parking charges. 😤😤😤😤 Remember this is the same guy that threw himself on the bonnet of a vehicle allegedly picking up in the drop off zone where the MINIMUM charge is £2.00 but also rises dramatically if there is a delay in unloading luggage etc. Dewar and the parking charges are putting small operators out of business 😤😤😤😤😤😤😤

12/03/20. So I have just been into Tesco. Honestly it was shocking they had no toilet paper at all. Reluctantly I headed for the customer service and asked if they had ANY toilet paper. .A firm NO and a look in disgust was the answer. Walking back to the toilets with my knickers and trousers around my ankles is a walk I never want to do again. 🧻

13/03/20. More deaths of sick, vulnerable and elderly is an economic plan of these Toly cunts....less benefits. They want a society based on cruelty, indifference, and violence. A pandemic is the perfect distillation of their core beliefs, really. A subtle, invisible agent that kills the frail, and leaves the strong standing atop the rest. What could be better than that? 👾👾👾👾👾👾

13/03/20. Why Britain's Coronavirus Strategy is literally the most insane mistake in modern history

https://eand.co/why-britains-coronavirus-strategy-is-literally-one-of-the-most-insane-things-in-modern-history-45c755f1db2d

13/03/20. Breaking News......both Trump and Johnson have tested positive .....for being deluded , megalomaniac complete cunts..

14/03/20. Johnson's is taking Corona Virus advice from his appointed Chief Medical Officer for England, Chris Whitty and Government Chief Scientific Adviser, Sir Patrick Vallance ....this is the same arsehole that appointed Not Pritti Person Patel as Home Secretary and Chris Grayling .....wait for it.... as Chairman of the Intelligence and Security committee......you could not make this up......Fred West Minister for Building Affordable Housing?

14/03/20. Trump and Johnson......if there is a God he will be on the blower to Satan....."I've got two more for your side.."......

15/03/20. Just watched a Dr Sonia Adesara on Sky News about Covid 19.....she reminded them she was interviewed on Sky in December and warned the Government about the need for action and the steps that need to taken......we are in the Middle of March and they have done fuck all. China built fucking hospitals in 7 days ....and Matt Hancock is asking "if you can build us a ventilator we will buy it off you at any price" Anybody know how to build a ventilator? pm me. In Italy the virus has killed 1500 people in 22 days ....she warned of the steps that were required more than 75 days ago. Johnson's advice..."people are going to die ...good luck" This Tory Government already have blood on their hands from the death of Millions of the sick, vulnerable and most needy in society with benefit cuts.......there is no doubt that the Tory plan is to wipe out as many of the sick, vulnerable and most needy in society with their obvious inaction and Herd theory.....that only works if there is a vaccine available at the same time.....there is no vaccine for Covid 19. If you voted for these cunts you deserve to burn in hell with them. Luv and Peace to all.....that deserve it.

https://www.youtube.com/watch?v=xkNcNvCJXP0

16/03/20. France just announced lockdown but with massive help for businesses and civilians....gas, electricity payments suspended. Johnson's announced the Tory's will offer payday loans at 1200% APR.

If you were selfish enough to vote for the cunts you probably don't think anything's wrong or even care

17/03/20. The UK Only Realised "In The Last Few Days" That Its Coronavirus Strategy Would "Likely Result In Hundreds of Thousands of Deaths" Scientists advising the government say an aggressive new approach adopted to attempt to "suppress" the virus may have to be in place for 18 months.

https://www.buzzfeed.com/alexwickham/coronavirus-uk-strategy-deaths

"We were expecting herd immunity to build. We now realise it's not possible to cope with that," Were you? Why the fuck were you not listening to true experts....not the stupid cunts that were appointed by an even more stupid cunt? 😡😡😡😡😡😡😡😡

17/03/20. To: UK Government   Tax dodging Virgin - no bail out!

https://you.38degrees.org.uk/petitions/tax-dodging-virgin-no-bail-out?bucket&source=facebook-share-button&time=1584453537&utm_campaign&utm_source=facebook&share=cb9b7037-cd7c-4999-81fb-6c5a45cee622

He has a person fortune on £4.5 Billion, The companies that use his brand pay little or no UK tax, they sued the NHS for £4.5m, and they've put staff on 8 weeks unpaid leave.
Typical Tory Capitalist Cunt.

17/03/20. Wuhan closes last makeshift coronavirus hospital as China's infection rate falls.

https://www.theguardian.com/world/video/2020/mar/10/wuhan-closes-last-makeshift-coronavirus-hospital-video

OK let's see how long this stays on fb....I was blocked trying to post an article on the slowdown of corona-virus in China because it "Goes against community standards".I complained and let it me access other blocked posts that I didn't know had been blocked including one about a secret advert for a £100,000 a year post in Edinburgh Council.....wtf is going on ?

18/03/20. Boris Johnson 'joked' ventilator appeal could be called 'operation last gasp'

https://www.thelondoneconomic.com/politics/boris-johnson-joked-ventilator-appeal-could-be-called-operation-last-gasp/17/03/

When Trump mocked the disabled journalist on stage I was certain it would be the end for him but these two pieces of shit seem to be immune to be taken to task for lies, racism and inappropriate comments.

18/03/20. Facebook is wrongly blocking news articles about the coronavirus pandemic

https://www.businessinsider.com/facebook-blocking-coronavirus-articles-bug-2020-
3?fbclid=IwAR3fQsH5S0J5cbvFiLq8h62GfS6Lc-wPTZsshgn3TOjHqmkv4TAlh7d9ZUA&r=US&IR=T

18/03/20. If you've been out panic buying, here's what to do. Take it back, with the receipt, go straight to customer services and say 'I wonder if you can help me. I've been an absolute fucking prick. I bought all this stuff I don't need and I'd like to return it. Could you also add me to the Wall of Shame entitled 'Panic Buying Fucktardian Cockwombles' and also announce my name over the tanoy explaining to my whole community what a fucking tool I am? Cheers!' Then go home and have a quiet word with yourself.

19/03/20. Does anyone know what species Ian Dumcunt Smith actually is? Is it simply sub human?

20/03/20. The Brexit assessments the Government didn't want released have been published – now everyone can see what they were hiding.

https://www.thelondoneconomic.com/news/the-brexit-assessments-the-government-didnt-want-released-have-been-
published-now-everyone-can-see-what-they-were-
hiding/08/03/?fbclid=IwAR1NQYumNETHQO498kwIX8uL2AHskmepOroFqqPpOovsylvwt4ZAkKTgN4c#.XnGR03a7rww.fac
ebook

This is an excerpt from their own study that they tried to keep secret ; "Brexit means far graver cuts and austerity lasting a great many years. If the UK leaves the EU on World Trade Organisation terms, the country is likely to plunge £120 billion into debt. If despite the contradictions that Donald Tusk detailed yesterday, the Government manages to negotiate a free trade agreement, the country will still owe an eye-watering £80 billion. A Norway – type agreement which involves staying within the single market leaves Britain £40 billion poorer" . So why was this complete bastard so keen to get Brexit Done....simple the £Billions him and his £Billionaire bum chums would make on the money markets.

21/03/20. Anyone that reads the political rants that I post will know I'm not a fan of Boris and think he was his usual dithering arsehole at the being of this crisis, however, I need to give credit to his government for the action they have taken in the last couple of day to assist the ordinary working and non working people of the country. (Still short of assisting self employed though). Bailing out the people instead of bailing corporations and £Billionaires goes against his grain but he's done it. The clown jester face was also replaced with the look of a man facing up to the incredible world wide crisis that he is faced with handling. The words come very hard to say....but well done Boris.

Nicola was her usual eloquent, calm informative self....but also showing the incredible strain of the situation and indeed seemed close to tears.

In the space of a couple of weeks most of us have probably gone from thinking this is serious but probably wont affect me to now feeling we are in some sort of apolitical horror movie.....which is nearly right only it's not a movie.

22/03/20. Coronavirus deaths rising faster in UK than Italy
The death toll in Italy from Covid-19 has now exceeded total deaths in China - the source of the outbreak. Could the UK be on the same path?

https://www.telegraph.co.uk/news/2020/03/19/coronavirus-deaths-rising-faster-uk-italy/

Very Very Scary.. It has now been two weeks since the first confirmed death from coronavirus in the UK - and since then the number who have died has been rising at a faster rate than in Italy.

22/03/20. Ah wis so pished last night ah canny remember gettin back from the kitchen.

23/03/20. Just watched Alex Salmond leaving court.....no big smile, no cheers, no gloating.......concentrated on advising all the journalists to go home and look after themselves and families. Well Done that man.

26/03/20. Let's see who I can upset with this one....I've spoken to McDonald's about them closing the Drive Thru's. Apparently it's because dispensing food to people in cars means staff breaking the 2m safe distance guidance. I suggested they use a simple spade to pass food across. They said they've tried that but Leroy wasn't comfortable being dangled out the window.

26/03/20. Fuck this. I'm giving up drinking for a Month.

whoops bad punctuation....should have read......Fuck this I'm giving up. Drinking for a Month.

27/03/20. How come there are still organised gangs of well fed Eastern European women with mobile phones still outside every shop and supermarket? Are they essential workers?

23/03/20. Johnson tested positive for being a fud .....and Coronavirus.... ..

28/03/20. Jeezo areas of Italy now starving in food shortages...gangs raiding supermarkets.

31/03/20. Going anywhere nice for your birthday......the kitchen maybe?

31/03/20. My thinking cap says....its very possible coronavirus was man made for use as a biological weapon. Was it released deliberately? I doubt this due to the devastating effects to the world economy and that the virus affects relatively fit younger population as well as the sick and elderly. If it affected only the latter then a population cull would be a serious possibility. However, there are very credible conspiracy theories about the moon landings, Kennedy assassination, 911, Trump and Johnson election wins, etc. There are others that do not fit into the conspiracy theory category. There is evidence of electoral fraud during Indy 1 and an establishment stitch up in the Salmond case.......but much more important than all of these ....there is irrefutable evidence that Rangers were relegated on the grounds of Religious Bigotry........and Big Jock definitely knew.

01/04/20. WUHAN RESIDENTS: CITY DEATH TOLL 40,000 NOT 2,500

https://unredacted.co.uk/2020/03/31/wuhan-residents-city-death-toll-40000-not-2500/

Reported Coronavirus Deaths :-

Italy 12,428 Population 60,550,075
Spain 8629 Population 47,007,367
China 3,505 ????????? WTF? Population 1,435,000,000
Russia 17 ??????????????????? WTF? Population 145,934,462

01/04/20 https://www.youtube.com/watch?v=PqbVLW8IYB0&feature=share

I've seen various comments connecting 5G, Wuhan and coronavirus but can't get my head round it......thought I was going to get the connection......but guess what..... "This video has been removed for violating YouTube's Community Guidelines."

01/04/20. On Tuesday afternoon, by the time Daniel Levy had announced that 550 of Tottenham's non-playing staff would be taking 20% wage cuts, neither players nor their agents had yet heard anything about similar proposals for them.

https://www.independent.co.uk/sport/football/premier-league/coronavirus-pfa-premier-league-talks-players-pay-cuts-nonplaying-staff-latest-a9439571.html

This is fucking sick and an example of how fucked up our society is...one of the wealthiest clubs in football cuts the wages of hard working backroom staff but continue to pay multi millionaires £hundreds of thousands per week to lie on the sofa with their games consoles

03/04/20. Trump says PM's coronavirus approach could have been 'very catastrophic'

https://www.thelondoneconomic.com/news/trump-says-pms-coronavirus-approach-could-have-been-very-catastrophic/01/04/?fbclid=IwAR2UAt2VyEaLJujiBbgt_JqHF5uLh756Q-Hj4Ft3SkAEbcepBKb9dZDwjEc

My life as I know it is over......not because I've got Coronavirus.....but because the most Moronic person on earth has just agreed with me about the second most moronic person on earth.....you know you are fucked if you start having the same opinions as Tronald Dump....

03/04/20. Anybody going anywhere nice this weekend? I might go to the fridge.....although the last time it was fuckin freezing......

03/04/20. I need to tell everyone before you read it in the Evening News......I was sentenced to six months in solitary (3 mths off with good behavior). I was found Guilty of being a complete bastard to every woman I've been involved with. This despite having a character witness appear on my behalf. The Judge said he was inclined to believe the 451 complainants rather than 1 hooker. The good news is that my cell in HMP Stockeree is very comfortable with large screen tv's in each room, large kitchen and a well stocked fridge as Kaleigh is allowed to drop off food parcels.

My old Mucker Bowser is in a cell just across the courtyard where we are allowed to exercise once a day if we stay 2 m apart......to be honest I've tried to stay much further than 2m away from Bowser since I first met him. I also have plenty to read as Bowser has lent me his collection of the Dandy and Beano....60 yrs worth.

04/04/20. Is the Weather Report at the end of the News just to wind us up ......WE CANT'T FUCKING GO OUT.

04/04/20. I was going through a pretty tough time recently but I realise was feeling sorry for myself thinking I was the only one suffering but quickly realised I was in a much better situation than many. That's not to mean our own problems are not important and can be easily swept under the carpet......but if there is to be any good comes out of this I think we might actually get a fairer caring SOCIETY....where nurses, doctors, firemen, shop workers, delivery guys etc are valued......and we realise how little the so called upper classes, sportsmen, film stars and especially politicians contribute to a SOCIETY.

04/04/20. UK overtakes China in grim global death tally of coronavirus victims

The pandemic started in China but more people have now officially died here despite the population being just 60million in UK compared to 1.4billion.

https://www.dailyrecord.co.uk/news/health/uk-overtakes-china-grim-global-21810433

China facing massive shortage of people that can count to 10........

05/04/20. Coronavirus: Police warning over Calderwood's second home visit

https://www.bbc.co.uk/news/uk-scotland-52171694

There is no way an apology is enough.....how many of her own rules did she break putting people's lives at risk? Resignation or sacking immediately.

05/04/20. If we must have a weather report at the end of the News why are they saying it's gonna be a fucking heat wave? Tell people it's almost certain there will be earthquakes, typhoons, hailstones the size of Trumps ego, a tsunami that will bring poisonous snakes and man eating crocodiles to the streets...... see if that will keep the stupid cunts at home.........anyway I'm away to look out my Speedo's...

05/04/20. Watched Contagion when it was released in 2011..... just watched it again.....OMG if you've never seen it now's the time..Stay Safe

06/04/20. Johnson in Intensive Care....nobody deserves to die from this virus ......but nobody deserves to die from suicide because of benefits cuts or people literally starving to death on our streets? He cut nursing staff left right and center and voted with the rest of the Tory scum against a wage increase to -NHS staff and other front line emergency services He put himself and millions of others at risk because of his bumbling buffoon act and starting to take us down the flawed Herd immunity path where sick and elderly dying was part of their sick plan before he finally took action. The government was warned on Sky news in December by en eminent Virologist about the need for thousands of ICU bed and tens of thousands of ventilators. He fucked an offer from the EU to help and said an email was missed and there was a misunderstanding. He did fuck all till mid March and Rabb stood and said "Can anyone make us ventilators please" before turning a fucking vacuum manufacturer. Johnson, Cummings, Gove, Rabb etc have stood in front of -cameras every day telling fucking lie after lie. You Reap What You Sow. Luv n Peace and Stay Safe.

07/04/20. The Conservatives have been accused of "economic murder" for austerity policies which a new study suggests have caused 120,000 deaths.

https://www.independent.co.uk/news/health/tory-austerity-deaths-study-report-people-die-social-care-government-policy-a8057306.html

Created by Tommy King using originals by wefail.art

Coronavirus has so far killed over 5,000 in the UK ....austerity measures have killed over 120,000 in recent years. Let that sink in. Luv n Peace and Stay Safe.

Coronavirus: Christopher Eccleston reads a poetic tribute to the NHS.

https://www.bbc.co.uk/news/av/uk-politics-52158721/coronavirus-christopher-eccleston-reads-a-poetic-tribute-to-the-nhs

07/04/20. Senior Tory loses it on air when confronted with his own plans to sell the NHS

https://www.thecanary.co/trending/2019/12/03/senior-tory-loses-it-on-air-when-confronted-with-his-own-plans-to-sell-the-nhs/

Lies, lies fucking lies.......never believe a word that comes out a Tory's mouth

08/04/20. I've been criticized by a couple of people for not showing some compassion towards Johnson even although the Tory's are responsible for 120,000 deaths from austerity measures and I stated I did not wish any ill on Johnson.. I hope they read these two statements and statistics......and then come back and tell me I should still feel compassion towards him and how he has handled this crisis. Stay Safe

08/04/20. Well said.....I think.....because even I hadn't heard some of the insults before. Description of Branson. "So here we are you granny grey haired leather skinned fanny fart of a spunk stain on the bedsheet of humanity

09/04/20. 100 Days that changed the world.

https://www.theguardian.com/world/ng-interactive/2020/apr/08/coronavirus-100-days-that-changed-the-world?CMP=Share_iOSApp_Other&fbclid=IwAR0WyN93Dje41_Rp7oj97NU8-GihNorkky9z9N8Q7I8Kvul__VanG61NCXl

Great read but a reminder of how badly it was dealt with in some countries ....especially UK and US. Mistakes that must never be repeated.

09/04/20 MPs have been offered an extra £10,000 each to support them while they work from home during the coronavirus pandemic.

The extra budget can be used to buy equipment such as laptops and printers for MPs and their staff, or to cover additional electricity, heating and phone bills.

https://t.co/kIUFoDEUos?amp=1

What the fuck are they thinking? How much does a laptop and printer cost? Does every poor self employed bastard forced to work at home not use extra electricity, heating and phone bills? I bet some of the low life Tory scum will be claiming travel expenses at the same time. Emergency legislation should be brought in to force every MP that is already a £millionaire simply because they are MP's to redirect their wages to an NHS fund.

10/04/20. Three nurses forced to wear bin bags because of PPE shortage 'test positive for coronavirus'

https://metro.co.uk/2020/04/08/nurses-wore-bin-bags-due-ppe-shortage-test-positive-coronavirus-12530286/?ito=article.desktop.share.top.facebook

Does our society get any more disgusting than this? Nurses risking their lives in fucking bin bags while multi £millionaire MP's get an EXTRA £10,000 to work from home. Parasites if they accept this and name the moronic greedy fucking scumbag that suggested it in the first place. We should get millions on the streets demonstrating .....all six feet apart of course.....

10/04/20. We are going through an experience that nobody has ever lived through. World wars, modern wars, terrorism, personal tragedies ......nothing compare to the world wide crisis we are in. This is going to affect everyone differently and our world may never be the same again. However, I am confident we will come out the other side stronger and I hope a fairer caring SOCIETY where we realise the important jobs in life are NHS, Police , Firefighters and also ordinary store workers and delivery drivers not Politicians, pop stars, films stars, footballers and reality tv show performing seals. A real society relies on ordinary people who are caring compassionate people. Sadly and more horrifically I'm still not convinced the seafood market in Wuhan was the source. Wuhan has been inextricably linked to bio chemical labs for years. The official deaths in Wuhan and China are ridiculously low and lies but at the same time they are recovering very quickly and manufacturing is already in full swing as is Russia while other economies especially UK, EU and USA are crippled and will be for years to come. Were China and Russia just better prepared and acted quicker? Or did they know exactly what was about to be released and had already protected themselves?

11/04/20. People are still claiming Johnson is a hero because he nearly killed himself by following his own advice. The Government he leads is responsible for the deaths of tens of thousands of vulnerable UK citizens before during and after this crisis. If we are in a war against coronavirus now there should be war crimes charges brought against them.....their inaction and advice has caused the UK death rate to outstrip both Italy and Spain

11/04/20. Non Pritti Person Patel says "she feels sorry IF NHS doesn't have enough PPE" IF, Fucking IF....nurses are wearing bin liners and being infected. Insincere lying Bitch.

12/04/20. Coronavirus: New UK deaths surpass Italy and Spain's worst daily totals

https://news.sky.com/story/coronavirus-another-866-die-with-covid-19-in-england-bringing-total-to-8-114-11971619

Anyone else still think I should show compassion towards Johnson who ignored expert advice in Dec 2019 on the measures needed to stop the spread of coronavirus. Not only did he do fuck all because he was listening to Tory advisers on the benefits of Herd immunization....sacrifice the sick and elderly..... he was continuing with "People are going to die ....good luck" statements.....boasting about going to hospitals and shaking hands with everyone. He did fuck all until it was too late and is directly responsible for the deaths of thousands of people including NHS staff putting their lives at risk to save lives....including this moron who should have been tagged DNR. I hope and pray that none of your family or friends are in the coronavirus statistics or the 120,000 his government killed with austerity cuts. Luv n Peace and Stay Safe

12/04/20. Johnson, every one of his cabinet and advisers must be held responsible for thousands of deaths and lying in Public Office which carries a potential life sentence. Johnson has already escaped this charge over lies when he was Mayor of London. He can't escape justice over this.

12/04/20. St Nicola has cancelled Easter....even Jesus can't come out.....her exact words were......"Now yis huv been fuckin telt.... jist stay inside especially over Easter ....Jist fuckin stay inside Jesus Christ......"

12/04/20. EXPOSED: Guess who used taxpayer funds to host the lavish launch of a think tank campaigning to let American corporations run NHS hospitals? Yes, Boris Johnson.

https://twitter.com/scotfreee/status/1249252409639153664?s=07&fbclid=IwAR1U2Zb4C0Lc O5mU5tPvF7DoWzFtzlxPhevK9sng8alJXI3-73PLtVjUYFE

Johnson has praised our NHS workers for saving his life and saving the lives of thousands of UK citizens. Maybe he needs reminding of the fact that he was using tax payers money and facilities to stab them in the back.

12/04/20. Johnson just thanked the NHS for saving his life and singled out two nurses to thank them.....one from Portugal and one from New Zealand........Get Brexit Done and stop immigration eh Boris you fuckin moron who clapped in Parliament along with Tory scum when they refused a pay rise for NHS staff. CUNT

12/04/20. This was the moron Johnson on 3rd March. The death toll in Italy had reached 450 in 24 hrs. Italy announced lockdown on 9th March and Spain the 14th. Cheltenham was allowed to go ahead on 13th March 4 days after Italy locked down. Johnson finally announced lockdown on 20/03/20 . 12 full days after Italy when the death rate was doubling every two days. Crime against Humanity.

13/04/20. Warning: there now follows a rant -

In the past 72 hours the UK government has ramped up its usual practice of deflect, deny, disseminate and is now attacking the very people who are doing their utmost to protect us and I am frankly disgusted.

First we had Matt Hancock insinuating that there would be enough PPE if people stopped squandering it... I'm fairly sure he's never had to wear full PPE 'cos otherwise I don't think he'd be suggesting folk are wearing it for shits and giggles given how uncomfortable it is. Maybe he thinks our doctors, nurses and social care staff are having fancy dress parties and making balloon animals out of gloves in all the downtime they've got at the moment

Next we had the ultimate 'sorry, not sorry' from Priti Patel, although I think her statement would have been more reflective of her true feelings if she'd just stopped at "I'm sorry if people feel"

Not to be outdone, Mattie boy stepped back into the fray suggesting that the healthcare workers who have contracted the virus, some of whom have tragically lost their lives, may have picked it up in the community. While that is technically feasible, if we apply Occam's razor, is it more likely these people contracted the virus whilst caring for desperately ill patients for 12 hours at a time with inadequate protection against a highly infectious disease or when they popped into Tesco to try and buy food on their way home from said shift?

And now we have bawbag in chief proclaiming he owes his life to the NHS. Yes, you do. Furthermore, you owe every person working in the NHS an apology for the way your party has tried to systematically dismantle the very institution that saved your life and belittle the amazing work they do day in, day out, pandemic or not. And you owe them a pay rise!

If you made it this far, apologies for the long post but I really needed to vent!

Stay safe, stay sane, stay the at home!

13/04/20.

In the year 2021

If God's a coming, He oughta make it by then

Maybe He'll look around Himself and say
Guess it's time for the judgment day

You Tory Cunts have had your say

Now is time for Independence Day

In the year 2021

Scotland's Independence will be won

There will be freedom from Tory rule for everyone….

13/04/20. Dyson £400 for a friggin hoover.....wonder how much they charged the NHS for a ventilator? I suppose at least some of the patients are picking up now........

13/04/20. You will be CH1PP3D! It's just a matter of time.

https://www.facebook.com/FlatEarthStationary/videos/233030051437813

A glimpse of what is coming .....and it's scary shit....

14/04/20. Is the lying, cheating moronic bastard Johnson capable of faking having coronavirus as a PR stunt? YES he is!

He named and thanked two nurses who "watched over me for 48 hrs when it could have gone either way" . So Johnson was close to death and would obviously been on a ventilator which is an invasive surgical procedure that takes months to recover from. But 4 days later ..on Easter Sunday when even Jesus stayed in......Johnson was able to speak for 5 mins without a single cough or pausing for a breath? Now I'm not expecting him to take a selfie and slap it on fb and Instagram but in this media mad world not a single official pic of him in a bed, in a ward, in a goonie...(sorry Tim RIP)...not even a sneaky pic taken on a phone? I smell shite......

Stay Safe and Strong Stay at Home and we'll get through this

15/04/20. Coronavirus: Trump suspends WHO funding and blames organization for Covid-19 deaths.

https://www.independent.co.uk/news/world/americas/us-politics/trump-who-funding-white-house-press-briefing-today-coronavirus-a9465401.html

Where the fuck is Lee Harvey Oswald when you need him?

A spokesman for WHO, Mr Pete Townsend said "What WHO? Who the fuck is Trump to blame WHO?"

16/04/20. Coronavirus New Zealand: PM Jacinda Ardern takes 20 per cent pay cut.

Meanwhile the UK gives MP's a pay rise and £10,000 extra to work from home......when this crisis is over....every one of this cabinet should be put on trial for their inaction, lies, deception and dereliction of public duties.

https://7news.com.au/news/world/coronavirus-new-zealand-pm-jacinda-ardern-takes-20-per-cent-pay-cut-c-977489?utm_campaign=share-icons&utm_source=facebook&utm_medium=social&tid=1586939506508

16/04/20. Please read this post to the end and share to end this dangerous practice.......why are Sky News presenters standing with their hands in their pockets? Got the belt at school for doing that.....

17/04/20. FFS just got a fixed penalty fine for going the wrong way up a one way isle in Tesco....

17/04/20. Breaking news.....Johnson spotted out horse riding........on Shergar and Lord Lucan was on the horse behind....

Not that I miss seeing the moron's puss on TV....but WFT is he? Why is Matt Hand Cock running the show? I mean it only took him three day to recover from being near to death to rising from the dead and giving a live 5 min national broadcast....without a sniffle , cough or a pause for breath. Now he's been AWOL for 5 days.

Still believe the multi millionaire leader of our country was taking up an NHS bed? No pics going in, being in or coming out. No interviews with the two angels?

Do you think if Trump gets the virus, and if he's paid his insurance, he will be going into a plebs hospital in a mixed ward? And I don't mean mixed sex I mean blacks and whites. No Trapper and Hawkeye will be commissioned and the White House will be turned into a MASH unit. Mind you Henry and Radar would do a better job than the US MORON in Charge.

19/04/20. Just watched Ian Dumbcunt Smith NOT answering questions about why 400,000 sets of PPE due to arrive today from Turkey has been delayed but several hospitals warned of Friday PPE would run out in 24 Hrs. He trotted out the usual lies that there was a shortage of PPE all over the world in EVERY country. Oh Yeah Dumbcunt....... then how come Turkey have 400,000 spare to ship over here?

He then refused to answer if UK sent 260,000 PPE sets in February to .....CHINA FFS.

He also tried to defend Johnson for missing 5 Cobra meetings by saying it's normal that a PM will not attend every Cobra meeting but could delegate unless an executive decision was required. There is nothing "normal" about this crisis and every Cobra meeting required decisions on preventing thousands of deaths. Are these decisions suitable to be delegated by the elected UK leader?

When this crisis is over....every one of this cabinet should be put on trial for their inaction, lies, deception and dereliction of public duties.

20/04/20. Boris Johnson ignored five Cobra meetings surrounding the growing threat of coronavirus.

https://redrevolution.co.uk/news/the-times-report-pm-skipped-five-cobra-meetings-on-covid-19-tories-ignored-warnings-on-ppe-austerity-to-blame/?mc_cid=63beb64684&mc_eid=a65d6ca41d&fbclid=IwAR0524gv5eJPyNYdsdkIbLRwfL Qbp7fM17YrTkIfGknGsTiLJ4BjyKfFnM

20/04/20. FFS we are now getting into Yes Minister territory ....Updates to the Nation on the critical issue of PPE supplies are now being given by the Secretary for Education and the Secretary for Media and Sport.....sorry don't know their names as they are complete nonentities.......are Hanncock, Gove and The Invisible PM now all out of lies and too embarrassed to update the Nation in a time of crisis? Strong Leadership? MY ARSE. Even fuckin Baldrick would have had a cunning plan.

21/04/20. Can I publicly apologize to Tommy Lee please? The sex tape of St Pamela of Baycrotch blowing Tommy was soul destroying.....I watched over and over again with the song "It should have been me" playing in the background......but I didn't appreciate what a well educated, intelligent and eloquent gentleman he was.

His opening of a letter to Trump "Dear f****** luantic," it starts. "At your recent press conference - more a word salad that had a stroke and fell down the stairs, you were CLEARLY so out of your depth you needed scuba gear" was pure genius and surpasses the description of Branson as " a wankstain on the bed sheets of humanity"

Maybe I could plagiarize both and address Johnson, Gove, Raab and Hancock "Dear f****** luantics" At your recent press conference - more a word salad that had a stroke and fell down the stairs, you were CLEARLY so out of your depth you needed scuba gear and I consider you all as wankstains on the bed sheets of humanity"

Luv n Peace and Stay Safe.......most of you.....there are exceptions.

21/04/20. I'm not complaining about not seeing Johnson's moronic puss on TV lying to us but he is the elected leader of the UK government and should be the spokesman for it not the Secretary to the Secretary of the Department of Pish and Shite's understudy.

A government spokesman, Lord Lucan said "Sorry old chap I've not seen the cunt either......although that could be because he was shagging my wife...."

22/04/20. Is there any end to the farcical but fatal mistakes this Government is responsible for? The testing situation is unbelievable. We are now being told NHS workers that had been tested may have been given the wrong results. Let that sink in....some testing Positive were sent home to self isolate reducing front line further but may not have been positive ....but worse some may have been incorrectly diagnosed negative and were sent back to treat vulnerable patients putting them all at risk of infection and death. FFS

22/04/20. Where the fuck is the Invisible PM?.....I think he's Potted Heed...Aye deed... deed as a BoJo...he was obviously seriously ill so the Tolies created a hologram of him to raise spirits on Easter Sunday....now he's actually deed they canny do it again because they will need to admit they lied to the nation. Anyone got any better theories?

23/04/20. UK had 'ample opportunity' to join EU ventilator and PPE scheme, says Brussels

They are killing people because they thought joining the EU scheme would be backtracking on Brexit. The Government said it was due to a "misunderstanding". The spokesman for The Foreign Office said it was not a "misunderstanding" it was a political decision. Now the Foreign Office has backtracked and said "I understand there was a misunderstanding understanding the misunderstanding initially and he now understands the misunderstanding he understands that the misunderstanding is now understood" Pritti Patel says "I've counted the misunderstandings and there were a hundred twelve and two misunderstandings as I understand it. However, I understand the misunderstandings have now peaked and I understand the misunderstandings will now level out as we now understand the misunderstandings"

So Lord Please Don't Let me Be Misunderstood ......they are all lying cunts

https://inews.co.uk/news/health/coronavirus-uk-ample-opportunity-eu-ventilator-ppe-scheme-2546863

23/04/20. I would like everyone that is feeling a little emotional and vulnerable know that they can call me anytime and chat for as long as they wish....I set up my own Coronavirus Helpline on 0845 999 999 ....calls charged at £10 per min.

24/04/20. Unlike the rest of you lazy bastards I've not sat staring at four walls getting pished watching Sewing Bee, Homes Under The Hammer and in James Baillie's case Porn Hub .... I thought ...right I need a work from home business....so I've started building yachts in the attic.........sails are through the roof already.....

24/04/20. Domestos....kills 99% of all known germs..........AK-47..... kills 100% of all known moronic US Presidents.......please?.

25/04/20. "Melania Have you taken your daily Dettol injection before going down there?

"It's possibly too scary to even laugh at this moron......we can only hope the morons that voted for him and are demonstrating against lock down follow his advice........that would be proper ersehole cleansing.....

26/04/20. Can Obama not simply declare a mutiny and seize control?

27/04/20. It's the fuckin lies I can't stand........I bought one of those Boxes of Wine......"once opened lasts up to 4 weeks"......fuckin pish......ah got thru the first one before tea time....

27/04/20. Got to say Johnson looks remarkably fit and well for someone who was close to death less than two weeks ago?

After fighting off the invisible muggers and taking his daily Dettol injections he is back to his full lying bullshitting self.

28/04/20. Coronavirus: UK failed to stockpile crucial PPE

Deaths from coronavirus in the UK do not include deaths in care homes and home.

This means the UK are heading for the second highest deaths in the world but probably the highest death rate per head of population in the world.

2016 - Ministers were warned about the devastating impact of a viral flu pandemic hitting the UK and urged to stockpile PPE.

Absolutely nothing was done.

Dec 2019 China reports first cases of a new flu like virus....

Dec 2019 Tory's spend tens of £millions on "Get Brexit Done" adverts but nothing on stockpiling PPE equipment.

When this crisis is over....every one of this cabinet should be put on trial for their inaction, lies, deception and dereliction of public duties.

https://www.bbc.co.uk/news/newsbeat-52440641

29/04/20 Government was warned last year to prepare for devastating pandemic, according to leaked memo

Some of the scenarios we are now seeing are truly heartbreaking and I suppose somewhat selfishly I hope it continues to be news stories rather than our own family and friends but that does not diminish the feelings we have for people we have no direct connection with. I could barely watch an interview with the surviving sister of her 37 yr old identical twin sisters that died within two days of each other.......both NHS Nurses.

I know this is where some of you will disagree with me ...... My tears of heartbreak, grief, sorrow turn to tears of frustration, anger and rage that are directed at the people that are directly responsible for many of avoidable deaths. Some will say "It's time to pull together and not the time for anger and blame"

No apologies if you are offended ....but FUCK that attitude. We are heading for the highest death rate in the world no matter how you measure that.....it is a catastrophic humanitarian disaster......that could have been prevented.

While Johnson recovered from his near death experience in three days to give his Easter Sunday broadcast to the nation looking remarkably fit and well he then required a further 14 duvet days to return to his job.

Meanwhile, we were subject to a production line of incompetent, lying stooges such as Non Pritti Person Patel who informed us of the good news that while deaths were rising.... shoplifting was decreasing! FFS in a fucking lockdown.

Why is it left to the normally equally despicable piece of shit Piers Morgan to slaughter our ministers and expose their lies and deception while the Bullshit Broadcasting Corruption journalists ask "How is our great leader and did he enjoy the grapes you took him?"

Luv n Peace to all that deserve it ....but Revolution could be on the horizon.

https://www.msn.com/en-gb/news/coronavirus/government-was-warned-last-year-to-prepare-for-devastating-pandemic-according-to-leaked-memo/ar-BB13bawK?ocid=spartanntp

29/04/20. Trump's next speech...."the answer is simple....and nobody knows more about being simple than me....inject Dettol daily and listen to The Cure"

30/04/20. The Guardian view on herd immunity: yes it was 'part of the plan'

It was obvious herd immunity was part of the plan but even complete numpties like me could read multiple articles about why it would be a catastrophic plan to follow

30/04/20. Just a wee warning about some fraudsters out there.......I was on my daily walk and came across one of them Poundland shops .....I stopped and said to the armed security guard "What's the story here mate?" ..."just what it says ...everything is a pound" he says. I said "so you're telling me this is just like a normal supermarket but everything is a quid?" "That's right sir" he says. Fuck me I'll have some oh that.....I grabbed the biggest trolley I could find and set off like Dale Winton on speed even ignoring the one way signs.

Well I'm just warning yea...what a fuckin con.......they've no even got a Beer, Wine and Spirits section.....

30/04/20. Is it too early to put up the Christmas Tree?

30/04/20. Nicola Sturgeon on Janey Godley

30/04/20. Conspiracy theory that Boris Johnson did not have coronavirus, *The Independent* can reveal.

Dumbnut Cummings......."Boris you've made a right cunt of this......in fact a blind plastic surgeon giving Theresa May a fanny tuck could not have a worse looking cunt of it.....but I have a Dumbnut Cunning plan to get the plebs on our side and make you look like some heroic war time leader".....Boris..."You mean like, like..er...like ...er....Hitler?......fuckin genius Dumbnut ...so what's the plan?" DC "right we are going to release fake news that you have coronavirus and are in an NHS hospital OK? But all the time you'll be in the back bedroom at No10 shagging Carrie's sister while you wait on her dropping the next Tory leach bastard child. Then 3 days after nearly "dying" you'll appear in front of the nation and thank the NHS for saving your life.

Then you'll have another two weeks lazing about "recovering" .....then Carrie drops Damian Dumnuts Johnson. The Plebs will love you. What do you think?"

BoJo.... "Dumnut have you completely lost your fucking mind? I'm the fuckin PM of the UK in the midst of a world crisis ....I can't possibly go into a plebs NHS hospital.....I might really catch the fuckin thing"

https://www.independent.co.uk/news/uk/politics/coronavirus-boris-johnson-andi-fox-labour-nec-hospital-doctors-twitter-a9464246.html

02/05/20. The real reason why the gov't is offering £60,000 to bereaved families of COVID19 medics.

This Government has blood on its hands.

Today (April 26th), it is revealed that doctors are preparing to sue the government if they find that conclusions to Operation Cygnus were deliberately disregarded. This is why all of a sudden there is a paltry £60,000 compensation payment being offered by the government to the families of those who have died as a result of exposure to COVID19 through a lack of PPE. The government has refused Freedom of Information requests to see the full document that even The Telegraph said was "too terrifying to be made public."

https://truepublica.org.uk/united-kingdom/the-real-reason-why-the-govt-is-offering-60000-to-bereaved-families-of-covid19-medics/?fbclid=IwAR2IAbCX1eYBvdxbIszzwiQ8VA0Z1H5ACQZ0sZbAh7xFQOivmitcFj4HbBs%F0%9F%A4%AC%F0%9F%A4%AC%F0%9F%A4%AC%F0%9F%A4%AC%F0%9F%A4%AC%F0%9F%A4%AC%F0%9F%A4%AC

02/05/20. UK government will not commit to a public inquiry on coronavirus response

What a fuckin surprise.....even these Turkey's don't vote for Christmas.....

https://www.reuters.com/article/us-health-coronavirus-britain-inquiry-idUSKCN2241QF

02/05/20. Johnson's named the Bastard......Cunt Jnr The Turd ...

03/05/20. Boris Johnson says doctors prepared to announce his death as he was treated for Covid-19

This moron is literally digging his own grave......"They had a strategy to deal with a 'death of Stalin'-type scenario" WTF? ..... Johnson said it was "hard to believe" his health had deteriorated in just a few days, saying he "couldn't understand why I wasn't getting better".

Well Johnson, I think it is hard to believe your heath improved in just a few days and can't understand why we have yet to see a single picture of you going into a crowded NHS hospital surrounded day and night with press photographers, a picture of you in a crowded NHS hospital, a picture of you coming out of a crowded NHS hospital or a picture of you going into isolation at Chequers? All we saw was a speeding limousine with blacked out windows.......not even slowing down to give a wee wave to the waiting press? Answers on a postcard to "Conspiracy's R US" c/o Royal Edinburgh Psychiatric Hospital where I am recovering from my own near "death from disbelief" attack. Luv n Peace and Stay Safe and Sane.

https://www.itv.com/news/2020-05-02/boris-johnson-says-doctors-prepared-to-announce-his-death-as-he-battled-covid-19/?fbclid=IwAR1i-YAskP-PW2APJm6-CCRI2_wdnItF7aMZHv-AGLwF4Z4VkG3vbAbsTg4

03/05/20. China lied to world about coronavirus and hurt vaccine efforts, leaked dossier claims

Whether coronavirus is manmade and was released deliberately or by accident may never be known. However, what cannot be disputed is that we cannot believe anything the Chinese State tell the world. China claims deaths are 4,625 and deaths in Wuhan were around 1500. Then the latest official figures released bring the death toll in China's central Hubei province to 3,869, increasing the national total to more than 4,600.

Wuhan has a population of 11 million, Hubei 60 million and China 1.4 Billion. So according to China deaths in the whole of China outside Hubei is around 800 ???? MY ARSE

04/05/20. Watching the latest briefing from Sturgeon and other Scottish Ministers and the honestly, transparency and feeling that they know what they are doing even when delivering "bad" news is overwhelming .....compared to the lying, bullshitting talking heads from UK Government. If you can't see that then it's not Independence we need from you ....it's another planet we need to put you on.

Interestingly on Sky, Surgeon was still talking and announcing how Scotland were going to introduce trace, test and isolate measures at 1pm when Sky news was due to start....but Sky announced they would be staying with Sturgeon. I quickly switched to BBC to check their 1 pm news.......guess what? Yep ....lying, bullshitting talking heads from UK Government. The **B**ullshit **B**iased **C**orruption.

04/05/20. Breaking News......Love Island 2020 has been cancelled 😱 If that news upsets you I recommend a Frontal Lobotomy.....although I suspect you've already had one.

05/05/20. There is light at the end of this dark tunnel......

05/05/20. Flights were arriving from mainland China, even though Australia had banned them six weeks earlier. Heaving public events were still allowed. A Champions League match in Liverpool drew a crowd of 52,000, about 3000 of whom came from Madrid, where a partial lockdown was already in force. More than 250,000 tickets were sold for the Cheltenham horse racing festival.

The only way to prevent 250,000 deaths was through draconian measures, the researchers concluded. Even then, Johnson would not put Britain into lockdown until one week later on March 23. By that point, many other European countries with a much smaller death toll had already been locked down.

07/05/20. Neil Ferguson: UK coronavirus adviser resigns after breaking lockdown rules.
So another top UK Government Adviser is another lying, cheating Tory bastard who broke his own rules for a shag with his married lover who was then going home to her husband and two children. Worse still he said he "thought he was immune" .....FFS is it any wonder that the UK has the highest death rate in Europe if the top scientific adviser "thinks" he is immune?

https://www.theguardian.com/uk-news/2020/may/05/uk-coronavirus-adviser-prof-neil-ferguson-resigns-after-breaking-lockdown-rules

07/05/20. FFS......how many more mistakes and lives lost are this Government going to cost? The decision to ease lockdown is now clearly being driven the people that put money before lives....Tory's. You can bet and trust that Scotland will not blindly follow.

07/05/20. Coronavirus PPE: Gowns ordered from Turkey fail to meet safety standards..

The UK is being led to a catastrophic loss of life by a lying, cheating moron that boasted of shaking hands with potentially coronavirus infected patients in a hospital taking advice from lying, cheating moronic scientific adviser that thought he was "immune" so it was OK to break his own strict lockdown guidance to shag his married lover. Matt HandCock stated that there was a world wide shortage of PPE but didn't question how Turkey were able to export 40,000 PPE sets to the UK and didn't notice the invoice was from Trotters Independent Traders (Turkey)

https://www.bbc.co.uk/news/uk-52569364?SThisFB

08/05/20. Nicola Sturgeon visibly emotional after challenge on care homes

Compare the emotional reaction and gentle response to her questioner by Nicola Sturgeon with the emotionless and angry tone used by HandCock and every other lying Tory mouthpiece.....

https://www.dailyrecord.co.uk/news/scottish-news/nicola-sturgeon-visibly-emotional-after-21985998

08/05/20. FFS ......how many more mistakes and lives lost are this Government going to cost? The decision to ease lockdown is now clearly being driven the people that put money before lives....Tory's. Do you seriously want to risk your life on the advice of a moron that boasted of shaking hands with coronavirus patients who takes his advice from a moron that thought he was immune so it was safe to break his own lockdown advice to shag his married lover before she went home to her husband and kids?

08/05/20 Calls for inquiry as UK reports highest Covid-19 death toll in Europe

Johnson, Cummings, Hancock, Rabb, Patel, Ferguson etc should be in the Dock when we get through this.

https://www.theguardian.com/world/2020/may/05/uk-coronavirus-death-toll-rises-above-32000-to-highest-in-europe

08/05/20. I hope we have reached a tipping point in Society........my gut feeling is that we will come out of this a fairer caring society ......I go out a walk every day and it's so noticeable that most people want to make eye contact, smile and just say "Hi". However, I also hope Judgment Day will come and the people that have failed us will be held accountable ....saving lives and giving every individual the opportunity to have a decent quality of life should be the priority over saving money. The Tory mantra of "making the rich richer and the poor poorer" should never be allowed to surface again. This is a world changing opportunity that we can't mess up. If it takes a Revolution then put me at at the front of being Revolting.

09/05/20. Lockdown Protests - The Great Awakening World Wide

Sturgeon is not wavering on lockdown but with mixed messages coming from England and Wales we are going to see an increase in people flaunting the rules in Scotland as well. On my daily walk along Princes Street it was noticeably busier and definitely more traffic on the roads. There is also a clear media blackout on anti lockdown protests all over the world not just US redneck states.

https://www.youtube.com/watch?v=2cmPhUAXsU0&feature=share&fbclid=IwAR3fgeyP5MH0 nz_YDBbKzRLNh5UMif_h2g0uGlDr8M0n3Rj2mgOHtlvBo9o

09/05/20. I am thinking about a wee bit of lockdown Nookie......following the advice of the UK Government Advisers obviously.....so any you lovely ladies that are up for it......and meet the strict criteria........own teeth and a pulse.....message me.

ps. from experience a Zimmer can be a handy sex aid....

09/05/20. Me and my beautiful girlfriend have decided after lockdown is over we are going to get married on a Caribbean beach ....and we are going to invite all my fb friends.
There's only a couple of things I've still to pick up ....first thing is a girlfriend.........

10/05/20. Anyone know if Samaritans do Home Delivery? ....and I don't want a depressed cunt to have a twosome with....I'm worried about my mental health and drinking habits. Two days running I've decided to treat myself to my first lockdown G n T.......but came back without the tonic. Today was the worst though....I bought the tonic and the ice and forgot the Gin........and I've had my once a day walk.

So any Good Samaritans out there? In fact I'm willing to change the criteria for any ladies up for some lockdown nookie.......forget own teeth and a pulse........ It's now own purse and a carry oot....

10/05/20. Coronavirus lockdown: The world reacts to Britain's 'incomprehensible' response, botched testing and care home crisis.

I suspect that at 7 pm tonight Johnson will give the UK advice based on Tory Mantra "Money before Lives"

Sturgeon will remain correctly of the opinion "Lives before Money" .....but the message from Johnson will cause deaths in Scotland as well as England.

"No country has been spared the ravaging coronavirus pandemic, but some have handled it better than others, and there is almost universal agreement amongst the world's media that Britain's response has been abysmal".

10/05/20. Does beating yourself up count as domestic abuse?

10/05/20. Anyone that reads my posts will be well aware of my political views ......some will agree , some will disagree, some will think I'm a total left wing socialist cunt.....and worst still a champagne socialist cunt.......with only negativity and blame to hand out. That's OK because I am a total left wing socialist cunt.....and worst still a champagne socialist cunt.........but I am also a loving, caring, socialist cunt that simply wants a caring fairer society.

I regularly post very controversial and possible offensive posts. Why? Because In my own wee world I want people to react and debate .....and be angry....with me ....or the establishment ...but in the main ...THINK FOR YOURSELF and don't be led by the Establishment media attempts at brain washing us.

FFS our Referendums, our Elections , everything that affects our lives is now bought and paid for by corruption.

We are now engulfed by the greatest threat to humanity the world has known.......but some people are still relying on complete capitalist morons to lead us. PLEASE THINK FOR YOURSELF.....and us

10/05/20. So in England the bad news is you still can't sit in an empty park, observing social distancing , not using cash, not using card machines, not touching door handles.......but the good news is from tomorrow you can now crowd into a garden center to buy a fucking garden gnome. Definitely an essential journey?.

10/05/20. So the world debt is Trillions and Trillions of Dollars or Pounds......who the fuck are we due the money to....Aliens?

Right here's my proposal for economic recovery.....we form the World Advisors for National Key Economic Recovery.....WANKER's and appoint me as Senior Wanker .....we wipe out every single debt and start again. Everyone over 16 gets a national minimum wage of £30,000 but they must spend it......no savings or offshore accounts......spend spend. Pubs, shops, taxis will be mobbed ...everyone wins? easy when you have a brain eh?

11/05/20. Sturgeon on GMB...Honest, clear, credible and statesman like .....in every aspect the opposite of Johnson.

The Forth Bridges

Magnificent. Trump paid a visit on the way to destroy more beautiful Scottish coastline saying "went to view the Forth Bridges ....total scam there was only three!"

11/05/20.

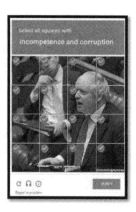 

12/05/20. Westminster website error says lockdown rules 'apply to everyone in UK'

FFS It's not a case of getting some things wrong......tell us when they get something fucking right...

https://www.thenational.scot/news/18440768.westminster-website-error-says-lockdown-rules-apply-everyone-uk/

12/05/20. I'm sure the Great Prophet had Boris in mind with this inspiration idea to change your name........interesting fact.....did you know Gandhi stated out as a lowly cloakroom attendant before finding religion and changing his name......yeah he was born...Mahatma Coat.....Now Boris why don't you go for Getyerhat Yercoat .....and fuck right off.

13/05/20. Kier Stammer has caught out Johnson giving a completely incorrect answer in House of Commons. Stammer said that the Government advice in February was that people in Care Homes were unlikely to get infected with coronavirus.....Johnson said the Government NEVER gave that advice and put care homes at high risk. He lied!

13/05/20. "Boris Johnson is a Cunt" song.

Right.....Thursday night after giving Clap to Carers and Herpes to Helpers .... I want everyone out on the street singing along.........

https://www.facebook.com/cal.jones.92/videos/10220356363248090/

13/05/20. Boris tells Keir: Pointing out that I'm wrong is not constructive

"Pointing out that I am directly responsible for thousand of unnecessary deaths including NHS workers is not constructive"......maybe not but it's fucking true....

https://www.thelondoneconomic.com/politics/boris-tells-keir-pointing-out-that-im-wrong-is-not-constructive/13/05/

15/05/20. Why can't they just say...."we were caught out in a scenario the world has never known and we are truly sorry for every avoidable death that probably could have been saved if we had taken earlier and more decisive action." I for one would have more respect and understanding if they were just fucking HONEST.

15/05/20. If Frankenstein decided to make a monster assembled entirely from human flaws – he would make a Trump........and with the leftovers discarded from humanity he would make Johnson.

16/05/20. My politics are left wing socialist but above all I am humanitarian who values life and a fairer caring society more than politics or money. It's also Nature or Nurture. Would Andy Murray have been the greatest tennis player the UK has produced if his mum was not a tennis coach? Would Jackie Stewart and David Coultard become world famous racing drivers if their fathers didn't own farms and garages? Would Tiger Woods have become one of the greatest golfers the world has seen if his father had not put a golf club in his hand before he could walk? Would John McEnroe have become one of the greatest tennis players the world has seen if his parents did not have a New York pad with a tennis court in the back yard? ......Would Jockey Wilson have become a great darts player if dad was a city stockbroker? NO! I was not born a left wing socialist with strong humanitarian instincts.....I grew up in an environment that nurtured these qualities. Was Boris Johnson born a lying, cheating, deceitful individual? NO he grew up in an environment that nurtured these qualities....as did most Tory politicians. How many pedophile scandals can you recall involving Scottish MP's or Celebrities compared to the endless links to pedophile rings in Tory PM's, MP's and celebrities? Nature or Nurture? Regardless of being a Unionist, anti SNP individual who would you trust with the lives of your family, grandparents and grandchildren ....Sturgeon or Johnson? Luv n Peace and Stay Safe.

16/05/20. Liverpool council defies government reopening plans – vowing children won't return until June 15 'at very earliest'

Teachers, unions, Doctors, Nurses, even businesses in coastal towns, and the dugs in the street know that lifting lockdown too soon is madness.....only Boris and The Buffoons think it's safe.

https://schoolsweek.co.uk/liverpool-council-defies-government-reopening-plans-vowing-children-wont-return-until-june-15-at-very-earliest/

https://schoolsweek.co.uk/liverpool-council-defies-government-reopening-plans-vowing-children-wont-return-until-june-15-at-very-earliest/

17/05/20. Matt Hancock accused of being a "liar" and told to resign.

The only reason that we are not getting the opportunity to see Boris the Buffoon lying through his teeth is that he is in hiding and trotting out The Buffoons to make complete disgusting moronic areseholes out of themselves.

Watching dead-eyed Matt Hancock talk about his fictional "protective ring" is a reminder that the daily press briefing is not about informing the public in good faith, but a crude attempt to control the C-19 narrative; one that has now departed from anything resembling reality.

https://www.indy100.com/article/matt-hancock-care-homes-nurses-pay-coronavirus-deaths-ppe-9518046

18/05/20. Great news at last....St Nicola has done it again..she has announced I can now play golf.......unbelievable as couldn't play golf before lockdown.

18/05/20 So Sceptic The Great Unwashed have been awarded 8 & 1/2 in row......SPL at it's useless and corrupt best...

18/05/20. Government advice is now to wear a mask and gloves when going shopping...wee Jimmy Riddle frae Niddry says "Ave been dain that fur fuckin years man"

18/05/20. More good news from St Nicola.....you will soon be able to go out and have sex with people that are not members of immediate family.......the Bairns in Prestonpans are delighted.....

19/05/20. How many more unnecessary deaths are we going to tolerate before Johnson, Hancock, Gove and their "advisers" are removed from decision making in this crisis? We are in an unprecedented world crisis and unprecedented action should be taken. Of course I don't know how this can been done but I can't believe those opposed to the UK Government strategy and advice i.e. every other UK leader, Doctors, Nurses, Teaching Unions, Transport Unions Care Home owners are not even discussing it? This is not a political issue it is a humanitarian issue. Should the UK Government be forced to form a Coalition of all UK Leaders and independent Scientists and Virologists? This is not my timeline below but it should scare you and anger you...

The timeline of failure by Useless Johnson and his incompetent minions.
December 31st China alerts WHO to new virus.
January 23rd Study reveals a third of China's patients require intensive care.
January 24th Boris Johnson misses first Cobra meeting.
January 29th Boris Johnson misses second Cobra meeting.
January 31st The NHS declares first ever 'Level 4 critical incident' Meanwhile, the government declines to join European scheme to source PPE.
February 5th Boris Johnson misses third Cobra meeting.

February 12th Boris Johnson misses fourth Cobra meeting. Exeter University published study warning Coronavirus could infect 45 million people in the UK if left unchallenged.

February 13th Boris Johnson misses conference call with European leaders.

February 14th Boris Johnson goes away on holiday. Aides are told keeps Johnson's briefing notes short or he will not read them.

February 18th Johnson misses fifth cobra meeting.

February 26th Boris Johnson announces 'Herd Immunity' strategy, announcing some people will lose loved ones. Government document is leaked, predicting half a million Brits could die in 'worse case scenario'

February 29th Boris Johnson retreats to his country manor. NHS warns of 'PPE shortage nightmare' Stockpiles have dwindled or expired after years of austerity cuts.

March 2nd Boris Johnson attends his first Cobra meeting, declining another opportunity to join European PPE scheme. Government's own scientists say over half a million Brit's could die if virus left unrestrained. Johnson tells country "We are very, very well prepared."

March 3rd Scientists urge Government to advise public not to shake hands. Boris Johnson brags about shaking hands of Coronavirus patients.

March 4th Government stops providing daily updates on virus following a 70% spike in UK cases. They will later U-turn on this amid accusations they are withholding vital information.

March 5th Boris Johnson tells public to 'wash their hands and business as usual'

March 7th Boris Johnson joins 82,000 people at Six Nations match.

March 9th After Ireland cancels St Patrick's day parades, the government says there's "No Rationale" for cancelling sporting events.

March 10th - 13th Cheltenham takes place, more than a quarter of a million people attend.

March 11th 3,000 Atletico Madrid fans fly to Liverpool.

March 12th Boris Johnson states banning events such as Cheltenham will have little effect. The Imperial College study finds the government's plan is projected to kill half a million people.

March 13th The FA suspends the Premier League, citing an absence of Government guidance. Britain is invited to join European scheme for joint purchase of ventilators, and refuses. Boris Johnson lifts restrictions of those arriving from Coronavirus hot spots.

March 14th Government is still allowing mass gatherings, as Stereophonics play to 5,000 people in Cardiff.

March 16th Boris Johnson asks Britons not to go to pubs, but allows them to stay open. During a conference call, Johnson jokes that push to build new ventilators should be called 'Operation Last Gasp'

March 19th Hospital patients with Coronavirus are returned to care homes in a bid to free up hospital space. What follows is a boom of virus cases in care homes.

March 20th The Government states that PPE shortage crisis is "Completely resolved" Less than two weeks later, the British Medical Association reports an acute shortage in PPE.

March 23rd UK goes into lockdown.

March 26th Boris Johnson is accused of putting 'Brexit over Breathing' by not joining EU ventilator scheme. The government then state they had not joined the scheme because they had 'missed the email'

April 1st The Evening Standard publishes that just 0.17% of NHS staff have been tested for the virus.

April 3rd The UK death toll overtakes China.

April 5th 17.5 million Antibody tests, ordered by the government and described by Boris Johnson as a 'game changer' are found to be a failure.

April 7th Boris Johnson is moved to intensive care with Coronavirus.

April 16th Flights bring 15,000 people a day into the UK - without virus testing.

April 17th Health Secretary Matt Hancock says "I would love to be able to wave a magic wand and have PPE fall from the sky." The UK has now missed four opportunities to join the EU's PPE scheme.

April 21st The Government fails to reach its target of face masks for the NHS, as it is revealed manufactures offers of help were met with silence. Instead millions of pieces of PPE are being shipped from the UK to Europe.

April 23rd - 24th Government announces testing kits for 10 million key workers. Orders run out within minutes as only 5,000 are made available.

April 25th UK death toll from Coronavirus overtakes that of The Blitz.

April 30th Boris Johnson announces the UK has succeeded in avoiding a tragedy that had engulfed other parts of the world - At this point, The UK has the 3rd highest death toll in the world.

May 1st The Government announces it has reached its target of 100,000 tests - They haven't conducted the tests, but posted the testing kits.

May 5th The UK death toll becomes the highest in Europe.

May 6th Boris Johnson announces the UK could start to lift lockdown restrictions by next week.

It's beyond me how anyone can still praise our government right now.

The lies and mistakes have built a mountain more than 30,000 bodies high - probably 50,000 when deaths outside hospital are fully counted.

And each death leaves a grief stricken family listening to the ineffective platitudes of Johnson and wondering what condemned this country to have such failures running it.

19/05/20. How many more unnecessary deaths are we going to tolerate before Johnson, Hancock, Gove and their "advisers" are removed from decision making in this crisis? We are in an unprecedented world crisis and unprecedented action should be taken. Of course I don't know how this can been done but I can't believe those opposed to the UK Government strategy and advice i.e. every other UK leader, Doctors, Nurses, Teaching Unions, Transport Unions Care Home owners are not even discussing it? This is not a political issue it is a humanitarian issue.

Should the UK Government be forced to form a Coalition of all UK Leaders and independent Scientists and Virologists? Please give some feedback and views.

20/05/20. Sturgeon has not missed a single daily update and given countless separate interviews...where she was emotional and drained but held herself together to give clear, decisive advice.......meanwhile.....The Invisible PM......

Nicola has been voted most respected politician in Europe during Brexit and now during the greatest crisis the world has faced.......meanwhile.....in England....we have The Four Arseholes of The Apocalypse.

20/05/20. I'm feeling good about one thing........after all these years of people crossing the street to avoid me and I can now go out and feel nearly normal......

21/05/20. fridge stocked up with 50 main meals.... according to the UK Government that is........ ..half tin of beans to honest people.....

Janey Godley - Big fridge in the Orkney's

https://www.youtube.com/watch?v=TwZd5lAHttA&list=UURvLN6EjLXIqteezXkpkU4A&index=86

23/05/20. My current number one of "Cunts you want to punch in the face" briefly replacing Boris and the Buffoons is Jackson Carlaw.

How dare the Tory prick try and score political nit picking points by demanding an enquiry into the handling of Nike conference ......an event attended by 75 people in February. Has he demanded an enquiry into Tory UK leader allowing 250,000 people to attend Cheltenham and 3,000 Spaniards flying into Liverpool during March?

23/05/20. Not only are the UK Government defending Dumbnut Cummings......they are accusing the Police of lying.

So we now have Police Officers who risk their life everyday in normal times being forced to risk their lives trying to enforce guidelines that Dumbnut was involved in making.

What reaction is that Police Officer going to get when he tries to ask a bunch of drunk neds partying on beaches this weekend to break it up ? Probably spat on

24/05/20. Dumbnut Cummings......Arrogant is too nice unless you add CUNT. same t shirt for three days and he goes to Downing St wearing it with joggers.....Respect Man.....NOT.

24/05/20. This government is simply a fucking disgrace. We need Kier Stammer to step up to the task and declare emergency legislation to form a Coalition of all UK leaders and top independent scientists.

24/05/20. Boris nearly died....what from lying? Did you see a single picture of the multi millionaire going into an NHS hospital? a single picture of him in an NHS hospital? a single picture of him leaving an NHS hospital? He nearly "died" but recovered from an illness that can take several months to recover from in 3 days to give a TV broadcast on Easter Sunday? Lies lies lies and now he has shat on a whole nation sacrificing saying farewell to loved ones to support the cunt that advised on and broke lockdown rules. There are no words harsh enough to describe him and his supporters

25/05/20. Carlaw is rapidly climbing the league .....currently led by Johnson with "Cumming ....and going....and coming" ...in second place......of lying cunts I would break social distancing for to punch fuck out of.

25/05/20 . Bishops turn on Boris Johnson for defending Dominic Cummings

There is a God and I love his messengers.......After Johnson's comments on Sunday, Baines tweeted: "The question now is: do we accept being lied to, patronised and treated by a PM as mugs? The moral question is not for Cummings – it is for PM and ministers/MPs who find this behavior acceptable. What are we to teach our children? (I ask as a responsible father.)"

https://www.theguardian.com/politics/2020/may/25/bishops-turn-on-boris-johnson-for-defending-dominic-cummings

28/05/20. As usual Sturgeon is honest and straight to the point.....and this is not political it's humanitarian. Everyone is entitled to an opinion but if you think Johnston and his boss Cummings have handled this crisis well don't waste your time or my time giving me your opinion. Johnson's statement that he was proud of how the Government had reacted and what they achieved is depraved and sick. They achieved the highest death rate in Europe 😡😡😡😡

https://www.facebook.com/theSNP/videos/961669931016087

Janey Godley – Boris is upset at me.
https://www.youtube.com/watch?v=Z4QRXd9xWi0&list=UURvLN6EjLXIqteezXkpkU4A&index=84

29/05/20. Students are angry at the delay in returning to Eton........Ben Dover, Patrick Fitzgerald and Gerald Fitzpatrick were outraged and said this was racially motivated and the activities of hate Preacher Soshul Distan Singh should be fully investigated.... 😂😂😂😂😂😂😂

29/05/20. I am really struggling to accept that no matter what your political views are that anyone of sound mind can show any support for this Government.....they are simply a deceitful lying stain on the bedsheet of humanity. 😡😡😡😡😡✂✂✂✂✂✂✂

30/05/20. Dominic Cummings, Boris Johnson's most senior aide, is facing conflict of interest accusations over a publicly undisclosed consultancy job at a healthcare start-up endorsed by the government and in pole position to receive cash from a £250m NHS fund.

OMG!! 🌐When you stumble across and realise the highly dodgy background relationship between Hancock & Cummings on the development of an AI Healthcare App going back to 2018/19, followed by the sudden government interest and the awarding of a £250 Million private contract to a business start up called Babylon, with Hancock offering to "help them".... you begin to see why this band of thugs and robbers are so perniciously super glued together. Worse than a rotten Columbian drug cartel!!! Is there nothing that Cummings hasn't infected, twisted, or tainted with his propensity for 'scoring major deals' from these clowns running our country??!!! 😡😡😡😡😡😡😡😡😡😡😡😡

https://www.thebureauinvestigates.com/stories/2019-10-11/conflict-of-interest-questions-over-dominic-cummings-job-at-health-tech-firm-babylon?fbclid=IwAR3dYvmDA71_PaukHkQiJNZkcN-IYVhEMnSfkJ45n9tFv13bX3BRDVc3j9E

30/05/20. This is one of the few un redacted pics..........remember this cop kept the pressure on George Floyd's neck for 8 minutes while there were other officers out of shot kneeling on him ......why? Was he a threat to their safety? 😡😡😡😡😡😡😡😡😡

> **Peter Stefanovic** ✔️
> @PeterStefanovi2
>
> At a time of national crisis, with UK having suffered the catastrophe of the highest rate of confirmed deaths from Covid-19 in the world, with millions suffering, many going hungry & at risk of losing jobs, it would be difficult to come up with a more comprehensively stupid tweet
>
> ---
>
> **Matt Hancock** ✔️ @MattHancock · 5h
> Thanks to the nation's resolve, horseracing is back from Monday
>
> Wonderful news for our wonderful sport

The cunt is so out of touch with reality he probably put £10 each way on Shergar 😂😂😂😂😂

31/05/20. Boris Johnson has prompted widespread ridicule after claiming he has never told a lie during his political career in a televised interview.

This takes lying to a new level...."I'm not a liar"...well you would say that because you're a fucking liar. 😂😂😂😂 Ask your brother and sister if they think you are a liar......in fact ask your father if they are your brother and sister.....but fuck but he's a liar as well...... 😂😂😂😂😂😂

https://www.independent.co.uk/news/uk/politics/boris-johnson-lie-career-general-election-brexit-itv-a9225601.html?fbclid=IwAR3KaJeuV3ljlaR6vv85rv7gHnA2hsmc_JLJiB_nPIbDlvkDJtJMJamjJDQ

01/06/20.

Wefail.art

Dominic Cummings is married to Mary Wakefield. That might not mean much to many people, but it is an important name if you want to know the state of play.

Mary Wakefield is of extremely powerful aristocratic stock which is formed of lineages that have been prevalent in the political world for centuries. She is a skyscraper away from Johnson in the pecking order of class structure.

Wakefield is as ambitious as many of her forefathers to be a success in the power play of the political world, and through her grandfather's involvement in the Monday Club (a far right organisation that formed within the Conservative Party), her backers happen to be the very same people who are propping up the current Prime Minister.

It is also important to note that Wakefield was assistant editor of the Spectator magazine when Boris Johnson was "in charge". When I say "in charge", I actually mean doing other stuff that could topple him if it was made more apparent what he actually gets up to. The more stable deputy editor Stuart Reid was actually keeping the magazine together, while Wakefield was learning the ropes from him, and keeping notes on Boris's activities. She is now commissioning editor.

The fact is that Johnson is not in charge. The far right pressure groups that once formed the Monday Club are. He is there simply because he has a private life that is so sordid and corrupt that he has been open to blackmail. And that is where Dominic Cummings appears. Johnson daren't sack him even if he wanted to. After sacking all the One Nation Tories who he could have used to anchor himself through Party loyalty, he left himself vulnerable to the more nefarious groups that are using him as a stepping stone.

Which is why Boris Johnson is putting his neck in the noose. He has no other option, because once Wakefield triggers all the dirt she has on him, he is finished.

Deaths yesterday across Europe:

Spain   2
Italy   87
Germany 24
France   52
Turkey   28
Belgium 42
Sweden 84
Portugal 14
Ireland   6
Poland   13
Romania 13
Hungary 8
Netherlands 28

UK ... 324

There's no way we are ready to ease lockdown & open schools

Peter Stefanovic ✔
@PeterStefanovi2

You have got to be kidding! You failed to hit the Gov'ts target of testing 100K people a day, have not hit that target on any single day, not once, not ever & for the past 9 days your own department has said it has absolutely no idea how many people have been tested!

Matt Hancock ✔ @MattHancock · 1h
So proud of all those involved in exceeding our goal of 200,000 daily testing capacity

Such a brilliant milestone. Thank you to everyone involved for all your efforts

We are categorically NOT being led by donkeys ....we are being led by moronic cunts that put profit before lives..... 😡😡😡😡 **Fucking lying cunts** 😡😡😡😡

Tweet

Piers Morgan ✔
@piersmorgan

UPDATE: We can't get a single Tory MP to come on @GMB tomorrow to defend their Government.
There are 365 of them.
Has there ever been a more gutless bunch of cowards in the history of Parliament?
One of you grow a pair - we'll take any of you.

19:18 · 31/05/2020 · Twitter for iPhone

01/06/20. Not one MP from an elected Government willing to appear on a fucking lowbrow morning TV news show in the midst of a world crisis? I disagree with Morgan though....it's genetically impossible for a complete cunt to grow a pair of baws. 😡😡😡😡😡😡😡😡😡😡

01/06/20. Coronavirus: No offer of financial support if Scotland locks down again

WTF......If Scotland decides it needs to lockdown to save lives...financial assistance will be withdrawn by Westmonster. 😡😡😡😡😡He must also be saying that if there is a second wave in England and the death toll escalates they will not lockdown? Money is more important than lives. 😡😡😡😡😡😡 If you don't want Independence after this crisis yer are aff yer heed 😡✂✂✂✂✂✂✂✂✂✂

02/06/20. I have seen Nicola Sturgeon close to breaking down on dealing with her multiple daily question sessions....but always remaining calm, clear and statesman like without ever avoiding trying to answer a difficult question.......then I watched this disgusting cunt laughing like the demented moron he is to try and deflect attention from yet another UK Government fuck up putting more lives at risk. Can you Imagine how the Scottish unionists would react if Nicola Sturgeon laughed and giggled as she explained the failure of the track and trace app ?

🏴󠁧󠁢󠁳󠁣󠁴󠁿🏴󠁧󠁢󠁳󠁣󠁴󠁿🏴󠁧󠁢󠁳󠁣󠁴󠁿🏴󠁧󠁢󠁳󠁣󠁴󠁿🏴󠁧󠁢󠁳󠁣󠁴󠁿🏴󠁧󠁢󠁳󠁣󠁴󠁿

"Johnson's darkest hour, his decision to essentially prioritise Cummings over the pandemic response, had at least three immediate effects. First and foremost, it seriously damaged public trust and goodwill in complying with lockdown measures, risking a deadlier next wave of infection. Second, it belittled staff and patients who have risen to complex logistic, clinical and personal challenges while delivering care. Third, it forced the government's scientific advisers into open dissent."

British Medical Journal (BMJ)

Wefail.art

02/06/20.   He MUST be held accountable. 😡😡😡😡😡😡

02/06/20. I can't stand the hypocrite but I give him credit for asking the questions in the straight talking manner they should be and expressing his views......to the point that not one Tory MP .....including the PM...is prepared to face him. This is a disgrace and press censorship to cover up a moronic PM that seems no longer capable of appearing in public but when he does is censoring questions that can or can't be asked. Welcome to Tory Dicktatorship UK.....NAWBAGS REAP WHAT YOU SOW. 😡😡😡😡👎✖

 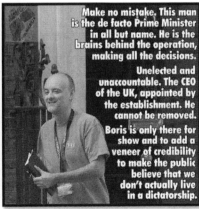

Wefail.art

03/06/20. How do you get rid of someone who isn't actually elected?

In theory, he's an appointment by the Prime Minister. In reality, he's an appointment by the wealthy and the landed... a corporate enforcer, or manager doing the bidding of the establishment. He is not accountable to the people.

I think people would like to believe that he can't be removed because somehow he has dirt on Johnson and knows where the bodies are buried. Unfortunately it's a lot simpler than that. Johnson is a bumbling idiot who couldn't run a bath, never mind a country. He is, however, likeable to the idiots who voted for him. Cummings is not likeable. He is, however, ruthlessly efficient... which is why he's in Downing Street to run things behind the scenes, while the clown show takes place out in the street for the benefit of the media and the masses.

03/06/20. Documentary says Boris Johnson told Italian PM he wanted herd immunity.

It's obvious that Johnson.......sorry Cummings......decided to go down the Herd Immunity route at the start......which is why the UK has one of the highest death rates in the world. 😂😂😂😂😂😂

https://www.thenational.scot/news/18490730.documentary-says-boris-johnson-told-italian-pm-wanted-herd-immunity/?ref=fbshr&fbclid=IwAR2UtehtZ6sIELsxHa5dao2BlMrnF8hnvDdVsOAkX4EpVUzlzarcYK2UusU

03/06/20. Johnson being slaughtered as expected at PMQT.....he has not answered a single question directly and is just bumbling and blustering at being faced with the calm, clear, direct questions especially by Stammer and Blackford.

And another thing if we are after truth and clarity why are they addressing him as the RT Honorable Gentleman? Surely it would be more appropriate to say....."Right ya lying cunt....."

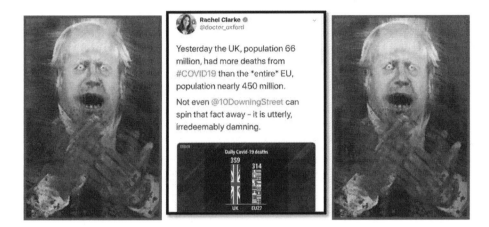

04/06/20. Yesterday Johnson boasted that he was proud of his achievements during this crisis ......that's the same as Hitler boasting about how low he kept his gas bill. When are the rest of the UK leaders going to come together and force this bastard to step down......or at least force Cummings to sack him.....

06/06/20. Now is the time to believe in ourselves and our Nation.

06/06/20. London protests: BLM Demonstrators clash with police.

The violence in London is horrific but I suspect that Black Lives Matter is not the only reason these people have taken to the streets. I fear that civil unrest will increase in the UK as people come to terms with the UK having the highest death rate in the world and we head for the greatest recession the world has seen. There are millions of people in the furlough bubble and not realising that when furlough ends they will not have a job to return to.

Before this crisis the Tory Government were directly responsible for thousands of unnecessary deaths with Austerity measures. Now they are directly responsible for thousands of deaths because of arrogance, lies and deceit to try and cover up their incompetence.

The high UK death rates are mainly due to the Governments initial decision to tackle the crisis with "Herd Immunity" strategy and then stumble from one mistake after another.

We are now seeing the start of civil unrest from the Herd Community. 😂😂😂😂🔫🔫🔫🔫🔫🔫

07/06/20. Arrogance, Lies and incompetence from the day these cunts were elected ......who is willing to be honest with themselves and admit to voting for them? 😂😂😂😂😂😂😂👎🔫🔫

07/06/20. FB Police at it again…..removing the picture of George Floyd.

07/06/20. Einstein said that insanity is doing the same thing over and over and expecting a different result..........explains why Matt Hand Cock keeps giving interviews......

08/06/20. Just off to work as normal 👻

Housebreaking and robbing Post Offices is so much easier these days.

10/06/20. "Disgraceful and shameful": Nicola Sturgeon launches scathing attack on Scottish

Tories

Nicola as usual being frank, honest and correct.....the Scottish Tory's are a disgraceful in trying to score nit picking political points when we are witnessing every day the disgraceful actions of UK Tory's.....

https://www.glasgowtimes.co.uk/news/18503284.disgraceful-shameful-nicola-sturgeon-launches-scathing-attack-scottish-tories/?fbclid=IwAR0PIOC20Ita_SVdPiaRskNGe6HxmKFJHni5puRW-N2HW6tZz6mRoJYeG9w

10/06/20. Sums these criminal up...this burds name...

"The head of the UK's Test and Trace Programme, DILDO HARDON, has refused to put a timeline on when the app would be launched".....OK it's really Dido Harding but misleading people seems the Government norm.. 😡😡😡😡😡😡

10/06/20.

So true ....because these moronic cunts are definitely fucking us from behind.....signed Ben Dover, Patrick Fitzgerald and Gerald Fitzpatrick.....

10/06/20. New Government advice....go live in a bubble......because these morons have lived in a bubble all their lives...

11/06/20. Lies, damned lies and Matt Hancock.

Handcock agreed to a lie detector test.....he failed immediately when asked his name....

https://www.facebook.com/watch/?v=262255108562585

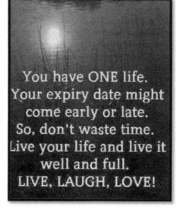

Can they still do that ?

Is this legal? 📧

13/06/20. Police and demonstrators "scuffle" in London. I'm all for that......if they keep to social distancing rules.....be like watching Morris Dancers in uniform skipping around..... 😎😆😆

13/06/20. The majority of the protesters in London may well have genuinely peaceful reasons for being there....but they are still in the wrong. They are obviously putting lives at risk including Police Officers forced to ignore social distancing to try and prevent them breaking the law.

As for the far right morons that were only there to cause trouble, vandalise national monuments and attack police.....shoot the cunts. We've had over 60,000 deaths of innocent, loving caring citizens.....who would miss a few morons being added to the total? Yours Sincerely The Voice of Reason 😎

14/06/20. This is one of those copy and pastes I truly believe... Great??? Britain 🇬🇧 is fucked...

... I don't give a Rats who this offends, but I stand by it. War is coming, sooner or later! You the Government!! You are all a bunch of cowards! You raised the cost of living so high that both parents are always at work, rather than spending time with their children (single parents stand no chance)😕. You took God out of schools. Parents were told 'No you can't discipline your kids'. Well, now most of those kids are rude and out of control. You shall reap what you sow! We have taken a whole generation and turned them into selfish, entitled brats who have no respect for people, property or authority! You deem people with terminal illnesses and some with only a few months to live...fit for work!!! You allow our veterans of war to go homeless and hungry but give out millions to foreign aid!!! You save drug addicts over and over again but refuse to give free diabetic supplies to those who need them to stay alive. You bend over backwards to be politically correct, too scared to say enough is enough, in case you offend someone. You put the retirement age up so people must work until they drop. You take care of prisoners and give them everything under the sun (food, medical, education, representation, money, and rehabilitation) yet you cause the elderly, those that have paid their debt to society and their families, to go broke caring for them either at home or in a nursing home... THINGS NEED TO CHANGE!

14/06/20. Boris Johnson to lead tributes at virtual service to mark Grenfell Tower fire 😡😡😡😡😡😡😡This must be one of the Morons most insincere vomit inducing speech yet. These Tory cunts never shed a tear for the victims ....but wept in the street because a fucking Big Clock didn't Bong. 😡😡😡😡

15/06/20. Why Is Dominic Cummings So Important to Boris Johnson?
Dominic Cummings is furthering Far-Right Libertarian goals in the UK, but his rich backers have also bet big *against* the UK economy and Dominic Cummings must stay in Westminster to deliver a No Deal Brexit.

Wefail.art

These Tory bastards have engineered a No Deal Brexit to make the elite super wealthy bum chums even wealthier while making the ordinary working class and middle class subservient rats in the rat race to keep the wheels of their roulette wheel spinning fixed for them to win at every spin.

The same bastards that at the start of the coronavirus pandemic took the decision to take the Herd Immunity Road......sacrifice the sick, elderly and poorest in society .....to make the strong stronger and wealthy wealthier ...resulting in the unnecessary deaths of thousands of UK citizens.

Johnson has already been charged with Lying in Public office which carries a life sentence only for the case to dismissed by one of his fellow Bullingdon Club Pig Fuckers.

Every single one of this Tory Governments Cabinet should be put on trial for lying in public office. 👿👿👿👿👿✖✖✖✖✖

https://www.linkedin.com/pulse/why-dominic-cummings-so-important-lloyd-hardy/

15/06/20. OK I despise Johnson as much as Thatcher but I doubt even Milk Snatcher would make these comments. This article has sickened me beyond my beliefs.

Mick North, father of five-year-old Sophie, one of 16 children who died with their teacher after being shot in 1996, said the future Prime Minister's comments made in newspaper columns were "callous and offensive" after he uncovered the remarks in the British Library.

Just read the quotes and tell me this disgusting piece of shit should be allowed to continue to kill thousands of UK citizens. 👿👿👿😢😢😢😢😢

Johnson has compared the banning of handguns in the wake of the Dunblane massacre to "nanny confiscating toys"

Johnson also pronounced that the massacre in a school gym hall demonstrated that legislating to control guns is pointless. 👿👿👿

After the government brought in a ban in February 1997, Johnson set out his sympathy for "the many thousands of shooters deprived of an innocent pastime because of the anti-gun laws demanded by Labour to which the (Conservative) government cravenly acceded."

He compared calls for a handgun ban to "the EU's eye tests for drivers of heavy goods vehicles; or the laws against bringing your pets across the Channel." 👿👿👿👿👿👿👿👿👿👿

17/06/20. I have a riddle: If you going down a river at 2mph and your canoe loses a wheel, how much pancake mix would you need to re-shingle your roof?

FFS are you stupid? ...Diane Abbott and Non Priti Person Patel got it first time......obviously because they both talk utter shite in riddles..... 😊😊😊😊😊😊😊✖✖✖✖✖✖✖

20/06/20. Apple 'not told' about UK's latest app plans

How fucking moronic do you need to be to lie in a national TV broadcast about being in Partnership with one of the largest corporations in the world ?

Actually I'll rephrase that ....if you are fucking moronic enough to lie in a national TV broadcast about being in Partnership with one of the largest corporations in the world .....you must a Tory Minister 😊😊😊😊😊😊😊😊😊😊😊

https://www.bbc.co.uk/news/technology-53105642

Happy Father's Day Jimmy 🖐️...46 years since I could say it face to face...😔🖐️

21/06/20.

Dr Kevin O'Kane @DrOKaneAgain · 6h ⌄
Note to @BBCr4today & other broadcasters.

Please stop referring to the failed "NHS Track & Trace App".

The NHS has nothing to do with it.

This was an un-tendered commercial app, endorsed by @MattHancock & given to SERCO to deliver.

SERCO & Hancock failed - not our NHS.

23/06/20.   That's my Christmas presents sorted!

25/06/20. Do you see anything remotely normal about this family pic? I'll go for an inbred family from Deliverance, The Texas Chainsaw Massacres.....and The Johnsons 😊😊😊😊😊😊

28/06/20. **"The Right to Hate"**. Not sure if FB will allow this but here goes. 😡✖✖✖✖✖

https://www.facebook.com/messenger_media/?thread_id=100005729436799&attachment_id=1524353257738778&message_id=mid.%24cAAAAB4LLV7d5LNWoY1y-5BfaR6pn

29/06/20. **The death of truth: Boris Johnson joins the ranks of Putin, Sisi and MBS**

'Johnson can only be understood as part of a grotesque and terrifying global phenomenon of leaders who regard truth as contingent and entirely unimportant'😡😡😡😡😡😡✖✖✖✖

https://www.middleeasteye.net/opinion/uk-boris-johnson-end-truth-joins-ranks-putin-sisi-mohamed-bin-salman?fbclid=IwAR3kL8kAFaleAvn6IHYaS2doO7UzTkzrT1bCoKyNmPxgd_efG7cU45SJgFI

29/06/20. Nicola Sturgeon accuses Boris Johnson of tolerating higher rates of infection.

It's Dumbcunt Cummings she needs to ask......he makes all the decisions.

https://www.thetimes.co.uk/edition/scotland/nicola-sturgeon-accuses-boris-johnson-of-tolerating-spread-of-virus-rqqblwtfb?fbclid=IwAR21Oah6c2BTnczCG1CQKfuJzoAIbfpClBWhOvmiW08xnzUkkdIgE-02hyM

30/06/20. Your FB Memories. 30/06/12. I would recommend the Blue Goose at Lanark Road for a great evening. Thanks to Gerry & Susie.

I knew this would be an expensive mistake......check out the bitch is already reaching to for my wallet.... I don't understand why God didn't just make me a farmer......given the number of cows that got me in deep shit....

02/07/20. Nicola Sturgeon voted 'most impressive politician' during Covid-19 crisis by Press Gazette readers

https://www.pressgazette.co.uk/nicola-sturgeon-tops-most-impressive-politician-poll-covid-19-voted-for-by-press-gazette-readers/?fbclid=IwAR2jr-57Twct1MzroLz1NKkYRFTOvBAs3gmwSv07J-jWFpoqTmnNphKYicY

02/07/20. No matter what your politics are if you can't see the honesty, passion and the desire to save lives in the daily briefings from Sturgeon you need to take a hard look at yourself in the mirror and ask " are my petty name calling, anti SNP , Unionist opinions clouding my judgment?" Luv n Peace and Stay Alive.

02/07/20. Rees-Mogg accuses Sturgeon of 'modeling herself' on Trump

This absolutely proves what a complete FUD Jacob Cracker -Mogg is.....it's Johnson and Trump that are hewn from the same piece of shit...or two cheeks of the same arsehole if you prefer.

https://news.stv.tv/politics/rees-mogg-accuses-sturgeon-of-modelling-herself-on-trump?top&fbclid=IwAR0BHFf2OLre9TTUiknPBO1sBu3sNSuY6a9oNvpLcZ_dTina3U5Vmyup6Oo

03/07/20. Tory policies have killed a quarter of a million people in the last decade

Austerity deaths and COVID policies have sent tens of thousands to an early grave.

No words. 🙁🙁🙁🙁🙁🙁🙁🙁🙁

https://www.thelondoneconomic.com/politics/tory-policies-have-killed-a-quarter-of-a-million-people-in-the-last-decade/01/07/?fbclid=IwAR3tGw36N9vKPU1mCY3hCtvWBumc5xULe7-MP2lOgMIE3slKuQFSNKRl6TY

03/07/20. Nicola Sturgeon has given on average 3 press briefings/interviews a day since the start of this crisis and quite rightly criticized Johnson's dithering and chaotic decisions. Meanwhile the moronic Johnson disappears for days and weeks at at a time taking orders from Cummings and leaves the equally moronic Hancock, Rabb, Pittel and any other minister willing to lie through their teeth to mislead the public and cover up their relentless mistakes and deceit.

Panorama on Monday night demonstrated that no matter what criteria they used the UK had the highest death rate in the world. Surely it's not an enquiry we need it is a criminal trial? Johnson has already escaped a jail sentence for lying while in Public Office. Every one of the lying cunts should be facing jail over this tragic avoidable loss of lives.

Johnson, almost certainly on Cummings advice started at outset to sacrifice the poor, unemployed sick and elderly with the Herd Immunity Strategy. Johnson is on record telling the Italian Health Minister this was the UK plan even although the ICU and Morgues in Italy were already past breaking point.....the Italian Health Minister pleaded with him to change his mind.

There is no doubt the death rate in Scotland is higher than it should be due to incoming UK flights with no quarantine, Cheltenham etc but with no restriction on these people then heading to Scotland. Johnson has already branded Sturgeons mention of closing the borders as disgraceful despite evidence of the spike in Dumfries and Galloway being as a result of cross border contamination. If Scotland had already been an Independent Country what do you think Sturgeon would have done at the start?

We live as part of the UK under a Tory Government that is responsible for up to 250,000 avoidable deaths due to austerity, benefits cuts and now coronavirus. We live as part of the UK under a Tory Government that will lie and cheat at every opportunity whether it be expenses claims, fraudulent second home claims, fraudulent salary claims for family members and now the Brexit betrayal and lies to benefit Johnson and his city bum chums personally while the general public's finances will be decimated. We live as part of the UK under a Tory Government that is responsible for rather that helping homeless people find accommodation they spend money installing spikes to prevent the poor bastards sleeping rough. Are you proud of being part of that society?

Many SNP ministers have refused pay rises and donated part of their salary for years to charity. Scotland's wealth from oil, whiskey, financial services and tourism has been raped and pillaged by the Westmonster and South of Englandshire for years.

If you do not think an Independent Scotland would result in a fairer, caring, safer and wealthier society in my opinion you are either one of two things.. 1) A stupid cunt or 2) a selfish, inhumane cunt.

Love and Peace and Stay Safe. 🌀✖✖✖✖✖✖✖✖✖✖✖✖✖

03/07/20. Boris Johnson repeatedly refuses to criticise dad Stanley for breaking lockdown rules.

Smirking, arrogant cunt that has supported Cummings, his father and other Tory's breaking his own advice....and therefore putting more lives at risk. 😡😡😡😡😡😡😡

https://www.lbc.co.uk/radio/presenters/nick-ferrari/boris-johnson-dad-stanley-lockdown/?fbclid=IwAR2jr-57Twct1MzroLz1NKkYRFTOvBAs3gmwSv07J-jWFpoqTmnNphKYicY

Post Brexit UK in January 2021...

06/07/20. 'Clap for the NHS': Boris Johnson joins nationwide applause on health service's birthday.

I still want to see concrete evidence that this moronic cunt was close to death in an NHS hospital. With the outrageous lies and deceit, we have witnessed daily for 3 months do you think it is beyond comprehension that Cummings ordered this fraud to try and gain public sympathy and deflect from the rising criticism of their failed Herd strategy and the highest death rate in the world? 😡😡😡😡😡😡😡❌❌❌

Created by Tommy King

07/07/20. The Prince Andrew Interview Deleted Scenes

This is Randy Andy The Lying Peodo auditioning for the role of Boris The Cunt at The Coronavirus Trials.

https://www.youtube.com/watch?v=r8Gq0qPMAOo&feature=share&fbclid=IwAR3aL6b_JQ-18rm94kLR36dmFtyAKDcsthwucgQPt6zPvffg3GS8EVumLjQ

07/07/20. Cummings to Johnson.."right you arse blame the care homes for not following guidelines and causing 20,000 deaths". Johnson..."OK Boss"

During an interview as part of a visit to Yorkshire, Boris Johnson said more than 20,000 residents had died during the outbreak because "too many care homes didn't really follow the procedures".

This morning Alok Sharma defended Johnson saying he was merely pointing out that "the correct procedures weren't known at the time".

Latest advice from BoJo Moron..."Right you stupid lower class scum......start following the guidelines .....and don't give me that "we don't know what the guidelines are pish......just follow them"

A racist, a sexist and a liar walk into a pub. The Barman say "What are you having Mr Johnson". Oldie but Goldie and always worth sharing........sadly it's fucking accurate and spot on.

07/07/20. OK went in search of Sweeny Todd but no barbers open yet....but I did find a Dog Grooming Salon....so now hair by Doggie Style. It actually looks ok but I'm not sure what he sprayed me with......every time I pass a lamppost I lift my leg for a pish.......it got worse though. Had a few too many beers in Raeburn beer garden.......last thing I remember is being on all fours sniffing a Labradors arse.......I was asked to leave but said I was welcome back......but I'm not allowed up on the chairs.....😊

08/07/20. First for 3 months 😊the only time I've been able to say that since I was 15 is when I was nearly deed in hospital in 2008. 🍺✂

Peter Stefanovic ✓
@PeterStefanovi2

Every time, every single time I think
this unscrupulous Gov't can't
possibly sink any lower it always,
always manages to rise to the
challenge

Free hospital parking for NHS workers to be
scrapped after coronavirus crisis

08/07/20.　　　　Fucking disgusting hypocrites 😡😡😡😡😡😡😡

08/07/20.　　　　Says it all 🙄

09/07/20. FB 09/07/15. Tom King "This is the society NAWBAGS voted for…'welfare reform' is nothing more than a polite, if a little clunky, way of saying 'strategically imposed poverty for vulnerable people".

5 years later 'strategically imposed death for vulnerable people' would be more appropriate. 😀😀😀😀😀😀✕✕✕✕✕✕.

09/07/20. Day 1 of the 3650 day plus challenge set by my maker……challenge is enjoy every day you have left😊😄✕✕✕✕✕

11/07/20. ………………………………Getting back to normal 😎😊

11/07/20. Chris 'Failing' Grayling as chair of the intelligence committee?

This is the political equivalent of having a kids birthday party hosted by Jimmy Saville and the guest band being Garry Glitter. 👎👎👎👎👎

https://www.independent.co.uk/voices/chris-grayling-intelligence-security-committee-boris-johnson-russian-interference-justice-transport-a9611831.html?utm_medium=Social&utm_source=Facebook&fbclid=IwAR1NsnUj4jUf4UuG5JvAn20e_u6-UTU2TQxQbYcjCHNJS5DFGiWH139Vxrg#Echobox=1594379840

11/07/20. Please read this and remember that the Tory Government said that maintaining free parking at hospitals for NHS staff was unsustainable. 😡😡😡😡😡😡😡😡😡✖✖✖✖

"£252m of public money given to Ayanda Capital, registered in Mauritius for tax dodging, to supply PPE that never appeared.
£186m of public money given to Uniserve Ltd of Essex, the UK's largest privately owned logistics and global trade management company, to supply PPE that never appeared.
£116m of public money given to P14 Medical Ltd of Liverpool, which had liabilities exceeding assets by £485,000 in December 2019 with just £145 in the bank, for PPE that never appeared.
£108m of public money given to PestFix, with 16 employees and net assets of £19,000, for PPE that never appeared.
£14.2m and a subsequent £93.2m of public money given to Clandeboye Agencies Ltd, a confectionery wholesaler in Co Antrim, for PPE that never appeared.
£40m of public money given to Medicine Box Ltd of Sutton-in-Ashfield, despite having assets of just £6,000 in March, for PPE that never appeared.
£32m and a subsequent £16m of public money given to Initia Ventures Ltd, filed for dormancy in January this year, for PPE that never appeared.
£28m of public money given to Monarch Acoustics Ltd of Nottingham, makers of shop and office furniture, for PPE that never appeared.
£25m of public money given to Luxe Lifestyle Ltd, to supply garments for biological or chemical protection to the NHS. According to Companies House, the business was incorporated by fashion designer Karen Brost in November 2018. It appears to have no employees, no assets and no turnover.
£18.4m of public money given to Aventis Solutions Ltd of Wilmslow, with just £322 in assets, for PPE that never appeared.
£10m of public money given to Medco Solutions Ltd, incorporated on 26 March (three days after lockdown) with a share capital of just £2, for PPE that never appeared.
£1.1m of public money given to Bristol shoemaker Toffeln Ltd, had seemingly never supplied any PPE whatsoever in the past, for PPE that never appeared.

£825,000 of public money given to MGP Advisory, described as a venture and development capital business that was in danger of being struck off the companies register for failing to file accounts, for no one knows what...

Meanwhile the nurses and carers, of whom over 300 have died whilst trying to save over 65,000 lives that have now been lost, had to resort to wearing bin bags."
Help Out and Eat Out get a Tenner off a Nandos and shut the fuck up, serfs.

13/07/20 ....SNAP.

> **Rachael Swindon**
> @Rachael_Swindon
>
> Ireland managed to get their track and trace app done for £850,000 - and it works.
>
> Boris Johnson gave £11 million to a pair of Dominic Cummings old Vote Leave buddies for our app - and it doesn't work.
>
> Why do they have to be so blatantly corrupt and grotesquely incompetent?

13/07/20. Because Dumbnut Cummings tells the moronic cunt what to do.....

Trying to kick start the business.

14/07/20. Jeezo BBC Scotland news presenter discussing the potential winter spike in flu and Coronavirus deaths reaching 175,000....."but it's not a dead cert"......it fucking is if you are one of the 175,000 😳😳😳😳

15/07/20. WOW. I'm going to use my Brexit Dividend to set up a Ferry company with no ships and a PPE manufacturing company that doesn't manufacture then I'll get £Billions of Government contracts........but please don't tell anyone......I don't want any stupid bastard ruining my clever plans. 😳😳😳😳😳😳😳

Claim your Brexit Dividend

As you are no doubt aware, British people are due to receive a massive Brexit dividend.

To ensure that you are allocated your money quickly please fill in your payment details below.

Name

Credit card number

Expiry Date   Security code

Mother's maiden name

* A small test payment will be taken from your account by JRM enterprises to ensure your details are genuine, but this is nothing to be concerned about.

ARE FABRIC MASKS SENSIBLE?
I WILL TRY TO EXPLAIN IT.

IF WE ALL ARE RUNNING AROUND NAKED AND SOMEONE PEES ON YOU, YOU ARE WET IMMEDIATELY.

IF YOU'RE WEARING TROUSERS, SOME OF THE PIPI STILL GETS THROUGH TO YOU. BUT NOT SO MUCH. YOU ARE SO BETTER PROTECTED.

BUT NOW, IF THE ONE PEEING AT YOU ALSO WEARS PANTS, THE PIPI REMAINS ONLY WITH HIM AND YOU WILL NOT GET WET.

Now, what do you think
ARE FABRIC MASKS SENSIBLE?

Tweet

You Retweeted

sarah murphy
@13sarahmurphy

What a cowardly, insincere, arrogant, dishonest, selfish, opportunistic, unprincipled, undignified, shambolic, tactless, clueless, rambling, lazy, incompetent, irresponsible, corrupt and hideous shit Johnson is.

07:56 · 07/07/2020 · Twitter for iPhone

4,962 Retweets **24.7K** Likes

Spot the difference. ✉   just pissed myself 😜   Couldn't put it better 💀

17/07/20. James O'Brien's powerful reaction to Boris Johnson's "despicable" coronavirus briefing.

By crediting the great British common sense when "his own hands steeped in the blood of British men and women, he's going to try and blame it on you," 😡😡😡😡😡😡😡😡😡😡

https://www.lbc.co.uk/radio/presenters/james-obrien/james-obriens-powerful-boris/?fbclid=IwAR1XsW8NdQDI7qKHuxWPsGlT-0i8oVlF1tHZyBJExbPUYKDKi_R7Ksi4qx0

> Johnson was the main instigator behind the group of Tory rebels who ousted Theresa May, claiming he would succeed in securing a trade relationship with the EU. 12 months later we are still in the same position as we were under Theresa May, and less than 6 months away from the catastrophic consequences of crashing out without a deal. During the general election he also told voters a blatant lie, by claiming he had an oven-ready deal, ready to go. What a sly man he is.

22/07/20. What a sly man? That's like saying The Moors Murderers liked a bit of gardening...😂😂😂😂😂

22/07/20. BBC CHIEFS SAY IT'S 'WRONG TO EXPOSE BORIS JOHNSON'S LIES BECAUSE IT

UNDERMINES TRUST IN DEMOCRACY'

WTF . The British Bullshit Corruption at their best. 😡😡😡😡😡😡😡✖✖✖✖✖✖✖✖

https://evolvepolitics.com/bbc-chiefs-say-its-wrong-to-expose-boris-johnsons-lies-because-it-undermines-trust-in-democracy/

21/07/20. Don't know what friggin day it is of the 3650 day challenge but I'm not giving up.😊

22/07/20. Tory's and their supporters are in inbred sub human species that would NOT sell their Granny for a £pound........they would smother her to avoid care home fees or worse claiming benefits. That was the case until Coronavirus "sneaked" out of a Lab in Wuhan and the Tory's saw their chance to eradicate the weak, sick, poor and elderly. Apart from that they seem a jolly bunch of pedophile, expense fraud KUNTS. Luv n Peace and Stay Safe.

Peter Stefanovic
@PeterStefanovi2

It will probably come as no surprise to anyone to learn that Tory MPs have voted down a legal bid to protect the NHS in a US trade deal. Has the penny finally dropped?

Tory MPs vote down legal bid to protect the NHS in a US trade deal
mirror.co.uk

23/07/20. President Trump wishes Ghislaine Maxwell 'well' ahead of high profile trial

FFS she is accused of pedophilia and sexual assault ....how the fuck do you wish her well? That's the moronic mentality of the US president.......jeezo can you imagine a UK PM awarding a known necrophiliac pedophile a Knighthood? ......woops hang on..... 😵😵😵😵😵😵😵😵😵😵😵😵

https://www.lbc.co.uk/usa/president-trump-wishes-ghislaine-maxwell-well-ahead-of-high-profile-trial/?fbclid=IwAR07YyG3Eia4vpqW5WG71H9HxRRlvu3XJhrNX3d2H7gAuxx-LJacbbBcOIs

23/07/20. Being of Scottish birth does not make them less of a cunt.......a Tory is a cunt simplze.

Every single Scottish Tory MP voted against Clause 17 of the Trade Bill, intended to protect the NHS from control outside the UK.

23/07/20. After 40 years of considering I was a functioning alcoholic the last 3 mths have demonstrated to me that I am not. I have an addictive personality whether it is good or bad for me and when I have a routine it's hard to break but I've realised I do not have craving for alcohol ......I have a craving for social intercourse.........that hopefully leads to sexual intercourse......any ladies out there that feel the same please message me......but don't feel excluded if you have a craving for alcohol as well

23/07/20. If this had happened in 1984 maybe we wouldn't be in the Tory shitstorm we are in now.

24/07/20. Brexit no-deal looming fast as EU warns trade pact 'unlikely' in furious clash.

Johnson said he had "an oven ready Brexit Deal" The only oven ready deal is firing up Auschwitz and putting these Tory cunts in it ████████████████████

https://www.mirror.co.uk/news/politics/breaking-uk-warns-brexit-no-22403499?fbclid=IwAR0Ro4UIYvvuiteJJzYYEkaoB-Ly55BBI5tTB2rbSxX_0tk-oVGpj3__0zI

24/07/20. Scots Gran battling cancer weighed just three stone at death after DWP stopped benefits

Please don't forget that Tory murderous austerity measures have killed way more UK citizens than their disastrous and deliberate attempt to sacrifice the sick, vulnerable and poor members of our sick society with Herd Immunity Strategy. ████████████████████

https://www.dailyrecord.co.uk/news/scottish-news/scots-gran-battling-cancer-weighed-22405870?fbclid=IwAR3xoyzxJbGxzUD55iVDR4pf9g7TwNbHtlFUxdjo9DejpoN_Zp1ZOUq5gLo

Breaking News. Due to spikes in coronavirus the UK Government advise following the new Sheep Herding Immunity Strategy measures MUST be strictly adhered to but are voluntary and fines will be issued if they can be arsed policing them.

If you are outdoors always stay indoors.
Please go to work as normal if you don't have a fuckin job.
Only drive if it is an emergency or if you fancy a McDonalds but wear eye coverings at all times. Available at all Dumbnut Cummings outlets.
Only work from home if you are a Muslim Suicide Bomber or if you're Fred West.
If you want a two week holiday in Spain quarantine for two weeks in the UK where the rate of infection is much higher than Spain.
You can have sex with complete strangers but always wear a mask and ensure you have enough cable ties or alternatively choose a recently deceased victim.

If you need clarification on any of the above below please tune in to regular updates on Radio 5 by the Government Minister for Free Speech Sir Marcel Marceau. The broadcasts will also be available in Braille for the Hard of Hearing immediately after the amazing specially commissioned by the BBC Radio performances by The Chinese State Acrobat Troupe.

If you need any further clarification of the below above just remember some of you voted for a Monoric Lying Cheating Cunt to Govern the UK. You Reap What You Sow. 🌀✖✖✖✖✖✖✖

26/07/20, Jeff Bezos Adds Record $13 Billion in Single Day to Fortune.

We need to reward Enterprise and vision but we are one sick motherfucker society when one man can accumulate this amount of wealth while children starve to death in every country in the world including in the USA and UK. 😊😊😊😊😊😊😊😊😊😡😡😡😡😡😡😡😡

https://www.bloomberg.com/news/articles/2020-07-20/jeff-bezos-adds-record-13-billion-in-single-day-to-his-fortune?utm_content=business&utm_source=twitter&utm_medium=social&utm_campaign=socialflow-organic&cmpid=socialflow-twitter-business&fbclid=IwAR0HnnsqfAaTwZOx-UN-Z3WQigFjjI4I4Y3YjuiPdRh2V15shKN10wu7Xow

Jeezo star of Gone With The Wind Olivia De Havilland has died aged 104. How long before the KKK and EDL blame BLM? 😎

28/07/20. Remember if your Granny dies only 20 people can show their respects but have the wake at the Oval where 1,000 people can attend..... and Morris Dancing is exempt for social distancing. 😡😡

28/07/20. We might now in serious danger of running out of "you could not make this shit up " scenarios. Sir Failing Grayling .....yeah the guy with no Dignity never mind a ship called that... is now UK Senior Security Adviser. Now Dumbnut Cummings who advises testing your eyesight by taking the wife and kids for a drive ......yeah that 'Vote Leave' cunt with a track record of misusing data who fists BlowJob before every press conference to make his lips move who is now effectively our Prime Minister - has just been given control over all government data. In the words of BlowJob......"people are going to die"......let's hope and pray these two cunts are next. 😡😡

28/07/20. Further job losses announced in Edinburgh due to Covid and lockdown......thousands of Romanian street beggars are set to lose their jobs. One called Ivana Geezapounski who didn't want to be named said the "trade has collapsed ...even though my Boss Tomski Kinski got me contactless machine......how am I supposed to feed his 5 kids, a dug and get a new iPhone on UC"? (Lucky I speak Romanian) 😂😂

28/07/20. BY Law you have to turn headlights on when it's raining in Sweden. How the fuck do I know when it's raining in Sweden?? 😎🌧

29/07/20. None of us should be politicising this pandemic

As usual Sturgeon is honest and straight to the point.....and this is not political it's humanitarian. Everyone is entitled to an opinion but if you think Johnston and his boss Cummings have handled this crisis well don't waste your time or my time giving me your opinion. Johnson's statement that he was proud of how the Government had reacted and what they achieved is depraved and sick. They achieved the highest death rate in Europe 😡😡😡😡

https://www.facebook.com/theSNP/videos/961669931016087

EDINBURGH AND SURROUNDING AREA LOCKDOWN PROTOCOL

DALKEITH - you are able to fight your neighbour providing you wear a mask and social distancing rules are adhered to.

PRESTONPANS -burgling homes in your local area is permitted providing you sanitise before and after the offence. Track and trace technology must also be used.

NIDDRIE -you can only visit your dealer when collecting your children from school. The dealer should wear a face visor and make sure all bags are sanitised.

GORGIE -having sex with your sister is permitted but you must be home before 10pm and use approved lubricant.

PILTON -Vigilante groups of no more than six allowed outdoors and socially distancing between the hours of 10pm - 2am only. You must wear suitable PPE for any physical contact.

LEITH - massage parlours are permitted to remain open, this is now classed as essential services for fear of the economic collapse of the town. Entry from the rear only

WESTER HAILES - now declared a NO GO ZONE (in 1984), if you must travel to this area please follow all diversions, traffic cones and signals, remain in your car, do not abandon your car, masks are not required as nothing is open

KINGDOM OF FIFE - everyone must remain at home and self isolate until manufacturers can distribute gloves with 6 fingers. Please do not go to A&E for digit removal as they are a tad busy.

MORNINGSIDE - a local woman claims she has a potion to "cure all ills". She may be home she may not? She probably has a better success rate with it than others so it's worth a shot, remember it's a "click & collect" service only.

GILMERTON - covid in these parts does not exist, therefore you should carry on as you were, house hopping, social gatherings, drunken parties and fireworks until January are mandatory, Survival of the fittest, and we're currently testing "herd immunity" in these areas.

Stick to these guidelines and we'll get through it together

30/07/20. When are any of these moronic cunts going to be charged with Lying in Public Office and face the life sentence it carries? How many millions of UK citizens face a life sentence of misery and poverty because of their lies and policies ? 😡😡😡
Boris Johnson has been caught lying, again! A recent investigation has found that Boris's Johnson's claims on how much care home staff and residents had been tested for COVID-19, were untrue!

https://voicebritannia.co.uk/boris-johnson-caught-lying-again-fullf/?fbclid=IwAR1klhWwMHxjn5EviJPAbjewvbMfWhYqgD-RT89_4QjDtPexgGGkJHZbpvI

30/07/20. No brainer ......Trump......

30/07/20. Boris Johnson boasts 'massive success' over coronavirus deaths despite worst rate in Europe

On a par with Shipman boasting of helping keeping prescription charges down or Fred West boasting he invented working from home...🤮🤮🤮🤮🤮🤮🤮🤮❌❌❌

https://www.mirror.co.uk/news/politics/breaking-boris-johnson-boasts-massive-22442631?utm_source=facebook.com&utm_medium=social&utm_campaign=mirror_politics&fbclid=IwAR3vWSu_MS7540Z4TdtOdxNKpOHmrxvLaw1_RbCUd13TomnGJ4-7zLZyFg

31/07/20. Fuck off Clownciler McVey. Trams were never necessary in the first place and its extension down Leith Walk is certainly not going to be necessary now with tens of thousands of Edinburgh citizens either working from home or not working at all. Trams will be as redundant as your brain cells always have been. Stop NOW and put the £hundreds of millions towards helping poor and homeless citizens. 😂😂😂😂

31/07/20. Jackson Carlaw quits as Scottish Conservative leader

Can't wait to find out what this piece of shit has been caught out with? Driving wearing an eye mask to bump into Dumbnut Cummings in Barnet Castle? Or just for being another Toly Kunt...💋❌❌❌❌

01/08/20. Morning after: Boris Johnson recovers from Lebedev's exotic Italian party

We would call it the walk of shame but this cunt has no shame...

01/08/20. SFA have just declared Celtic league champions 2020/21. With two Asterix Titles in a row Sceptic have now won more asterix titles than any other club in world football. 😂😂

Janey Godley - Emotional life jackets

https://www.youtube.com/watch?v=IBCpQhe_kZ4&list=UURvLN6EjLXIqteezXkpkU4A&index=78

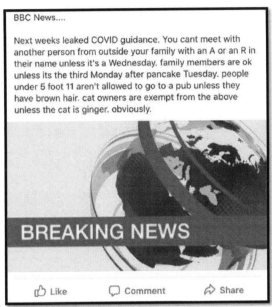

BBC News....

Next weeks leaked COVID guidance. You cant meet with another person from outside your family with an A or an R in their name unless it's a Wednesday. family members are ok unless its the third Monday after pancake Tuesday. people under 5 foot 11 aren't allowed to go to a pub unless they have brown hair. cat owners are exempt from the above unless the cat is ginger. obviously.

BREAKING NEWS

👍 Like   💬 Comment   ↪ Share

02/08/20. My son Josh was on the phone and said "Dad I'm a bit worried about your stress levels why don't you try medication every day?" Ok Josh but the only medication I trust is alcohol but happy to take your advice and I'll go on a 3650 day challenge. Turns out he said "meditation "😑😑

03/08/20. Toly Coronavirus helpline recording "Hi my name is Diane Abbott MP......should I wear a mask when on line shopping? ....."of course you should Ms Abbott....for two reasons.....it's a well known fact that the deadly coronavirus is spread directly through the 5G -network in Wuhan.....the second reason is that you are a stupid cunt" ✖✖✖✖✖✖✖

Janey Godley – You were TELT

https://www.youtube.com/watch?v=HNvWj9OPA7k&list=UURvLN6EjLXIqteezXkpkU4A&index=75

3/08/20. I will never understand the mentality of people who vote conservative. Who would vote for this? So many 'Lords' of this country live overseas. We have the largest unelected chamber outside communist China. Why do people vote for parties who sustain that, then complain about money being wasted on food vouchers for poor kids?

Our 650+ members of the House of Lords get over £300 each day - just to sign in! They don't even have to stay beyond signing in for the day. And they couldn't all stay even if they wanted to, cause less than 400 of them can fit in the Lords chamber. If that's not a sign that it's no longer fit for purpose, I don't know what is.

6/08/20. Sat down for a beer in the sunshine. Next table . ...attractive single lady. Eye contact and smiles exchanged....our seats duly moved slightly closer and polite conversation ensued. Body language and conversation was heading towards the start of a beautiful relationship..... or at least a fun afternoon. Then I realised lockdown has not changed one thing......my ability to find the only drunk mentally unstable female in the pub. 😩 Could have been worse... fun afternoon.... then Nicola announces a 14 day lockdown at 6 pm 😩😩😩😩

04/08/20. WTF just exploded in Lebanon?

James Kelly Retweeted

alispinner
@ACSpinner

BREAKING   : as outrage builds in UK media over the stupidity of middle eastern authorities placing explosive materials so close to a city, 4 UK submarines with nuclear weapons dock at Faslane HMNB base, 23 miles from Glasgow's largest children's hospital.

12:16 PM · Aug 5, 2020 · Twitter for Android

2.2K Retweets and comments   4.7K Likes

Janey Godley - Aberdeen football

https://www.youtube.com/watch?v=oa9JKeLHDcM&list=UURvLN6EjLXIqteezXkpkU4A&index=74

09/08/20. or the KKK......Konsevative Kunt Klan.😂😂😂😂😂😂

Magpie's View GTTO Antifa
@MagpiesView

Italy has the Mafia
Russia has the Bradva
Jamaica has the Yardies
Japan has the Yakuza
China has the Triads

Britain has the Tories

3:51 pm · 25 Jul 2020 · Twitter Web App

Hi I'm Liz Truss, the Tory Secretary of State for International Trade. I blew £150 million of taxpayer's money buying useless masks which can't be used because they don't meet safety standards from a hedge fund company registered in a foreign tax haven via a deal brokered by one of my advisors, Andrew Mills, who is a Senior Board Adviser with the company, **Ayanda Capital.**

9/08/20. Why are we not jailing these cunts? 😂😂😂😂😂😂😂😂

11/08/20. FFS...Coronavirus new deaths....Scotland 0, N.I. 0, Wales 2.....England "we can't release the figures due to technical issues".......i.e. we don't want to tell the world how much we fucked up and NON Priti Person Patel's abacus broke due to overload.

12/08/20. Trump says 1917 Spanish Flu probably ended the Second World War.

https://news.sky.com/story/trump-says-1917-spanish-flu-probably-ended-second-world-war-in-historical-blunders-12047035?fbclid=IwAR1nDm0sD5-IOASfzkCoPSsBWGxrRcpTTlRRtTQ6D7dlLwpl3hoBYiSfKNg

Can we please start a Crowdfunding Project to pay a sniper to take this moronic cunt out?

12/08/20. Sunak was asked why the GDP figures were so much worse than other EU countries...."it's because the UK economy is more dependent on leisure activities such as going to the cinema and eating out" What an absolute ridiculous lying prick. UK more dependent on leisure activities than Spain, Italy and France?

12/08/20. Wait till the poor suffering NHS staff need to pay for parking if they want their car back ...

Victoria Hospital staff car park!! 2020 just keeps on giving to the NHS. We're gonna need a bigger clap.

13/08/20. BOJO and the heatwave.

With highs of 33° expected AGAIN today, it's time to ask "could the government have done more? Downing Street knew about this heatwave weeks ago and has done nothing. Shipments of 400,000 pairs of Speedos and 5000,000 bikinis, sun cream and cornetto's have reportedly been sent back as unsafe after media claims the shipment was quarantined a month ago and Boris did nothing.

Karen from Chavington Posted on Twitter "We just don't know if it's safe to go outside and sunbathe because we can't function or think for ourselves. Boris hasn't told us either way and all my obese kids need ice cream and sweets. Hubby can't get out robbing anyone so we're out of lager and weed, I blame the government entirely"

Meanwhile, anti-heat protesters dressed in thick jumpers chanting "we can't breath" have marched on London, Big Ben has been removed and a giant cornetto put in its place by protesters.

The BBC reported, "Clearly the sun has come out and Downing street has done nothing to prevent it".

A second heat Wave is expected to hit England in 4 weeks time .

13/08.20. During the worst crisis the world has faced it's good to know McVeigh, McInnes and Edinburgh Clowncil are getting their priorities right. Apart from restarting the white elephant Leith tram works when thousands of Edinburgh citizens will be working from home or no jobs to commute to digging up their newly finished £6,000,000 on pavement cycle path in the process they have now spent unknown £thousands on thousands of pavement stickers telling us when to press the buttons to cross the road with signs telling us it's due to Coronavirus fuckin arseholes 😡😡😡😡

Janey Godley - Football again

https://www.youtube.com/watch?v=4qldSnaWDIk&list=UURvLN6EjLXIqteezXkpkU4A&index=73

Your Memories fb

.

Where did it all go wrong? a Roller, hunners oh burds, Breakers Hotel Miami Beach.....getting into Busters every night free....I spent most of my fortune on Budweiser, champagne, fast women and slow horses.....the rest I just wasted..... 🐵

14/08/20. So a day after Sturgeon and Swinney made unreserved apologies for errors and immediately reversed the system is James Stupidcuntytolynotcleverly going to apologise for an even bigger fiasco in English gradings? 😠😠😠✖✖✖✖✖✖✖✖

16/10/20. So Rooth The Mooth calls for John Swinney to resign but after a complete farce in Englandshire she calls for Gavin Williamson to "get a grip" ????? And where the fuck is a statement from James StupidcuntynotCleverly criticizing Williamson? 😠😠😠😠💩✖✖✖✖✖

17/08/20. Never ever feel ashamed about asking for help with how you are feeling.....being open and talking can save you from the torture.....I know

In the early afternoon of August 10, 2014, a sad and downcast man entered a snack bar. An attendant recognized him. It was actor Robin Williams. As several fans would do, she asked him to take a picture together. He did not deny it, but it was clear that he was not well. He was suffering from a severe depression. The girl must have thought: how a talented person, held professionally, dear and millionaire may not be happy? This was the last photo of him in life. On the morning of the next day the maid of his house, found him lifeless. The forensics pointed suicide. Depression is a serious illness. Often those who are close ignore the signs. Someone who made us laugh so many times with his films, did not deserve to end his story like this ... if someone asked: can I help you? Or would you like to talk? We would have another ending? Unfortunately we will never know...

17/08/20. The A-level fiasco shows why Boris Johnson is profoundly unfit to be Prime Minister

Great article. Simple, straight to the point and utterly destroyed Johnson and his boss Cummings. The fear is they are like Teflon Trump.....no matter how many times they lie, cheat or make disastrous mistakes the just ignore it and move on to the next disaster because no matter how terrible their mistakes are for the vast majority of UK citizens they will either personally benefit or it will not affect them. Cunts

https://www.newstatesman.com/politics/education/2020/08/level-fiasco-shows-why-boris-johnson-profoundly-unfit-be-prime-minister?fbclid=IwAR1L4827r3EZWEo4OxJTiZ58tAiFLweyzsAArh0YBNhNiSKmtIdQefaaQlY

Janey Godley - U turns

https://www.youtube.com/watch?v=otE5QyOI51U&list=UURvLN6EjLXIqteezXkpkU4A&index=

67

18/08/20. Diana Mary "Dildo Hardon" Harding, Baroness Harding of Winscombe is a British businesswoman serving as chairwoman of NHS Improvement since 2017 and head of the NHS Test and Trace programme, established to track and help prevent the spread of COVID-19 in England, since May 2020⬛⬛⬛⬛⬛⬛⬛⬛ THE UK IS TOTALLY FUCKED.........THESE INBRED TOLY CUNTS SHOULD NOW BE FACING CIVIL UNREST AND DISOBEDIENCE UNTIL THEY ARE REMOVED FROM POWER AND BROUGHT TO JUSTICE. ⬛⬛⬛⬛⬛⬛xxxxxxxxxxxxxxxxxxxxxxxxxxxxxxx

Dido Harding, a Conservative peer who heads up England's widely criticised test-and-trace system, has been chosen to run a new institute to replace Public England, after the controversial decision to axe the agency.

Health

The entire board of PHE was made up of medical and scientific experts.......Dildo Hardon was the Chair of The Jockey Club when Cheltenham was sanctioned to go ahead in March......The Lunatics are Running the Asylum. ⬛⬛⬛⬛⬛⬛⬛⬛⬛

19/08/20.

I know it might seem frivolous at first but there is a serious message. The majority of independent Licenced Trade outlets are on their knees and are not going to survive. Myself and a few friends made a conscious decision to support Le Di-Vin operated by Virginie Brouard even more than previously because her and the staff deserve our custom because of the quality and friendly service they always showed pre covid. Hence my fb check ins. I have recently been unable to get a seat at a table in a couple other of locals but I have also observed people taking up table space sitting chatting but clearly not spending. People if you want one coffee and a two hour chat then go to be ripped off in Starbucks ...do not rip off an independent trader by preventing people who wish to spend money by taking up space. I support independent businesses more than ever and will never set foot in a Wetherspoons or any other chain again. Luv N Peace and Stay Safe. ✪✕✕✕✕✕✕✕

19/08/20. Had an MOT at Doctors......she said I should cut back on alcohol to the recommended 14 units a day.......I'm sure that's what she said but I didn't have my hearing aids on....but I said I would try. ✪✕

19/08/20. Student who wrote story about biased algorithm has results downgraded
https://www.theguardian.com/education/2020/aug/18/ashton-a-level-student-predicted-results-fiasco-in-prize-winning-story-jessica-johnson-ashton?CMP=fb_gu&utm_medium=Social&utm_source=Facebook&fbclid=IwAR3G5We49qeB6rYYqSgvTe2LX4AH_U81M4XH2G6anc7NrutNeWB3qSGpLcQ#Echobox=1597780368

WOW. This is a must read.

19/08/20. Nick Ferrari asks Matt Hancock why Dido Harding is in charge of new health body

https://www.lbc.co.uk/radio/presenters/nick-ferrari/matt-hancock-dido-harding-new-health-body/?fbclid=IwAR0wL87oo8Ip9E_37tX-86EXLJXJGUbZPUksEWBy8O9C1ycEXkULxOeOIRI

"I note that the interim chair is going to be Baroness Harding, so of course has been in charge of Test & Trace, where we've seen that 10,000 outsourced staff have managed to speak to an average of two people each.

"She was also in charge of TalkTalk at a time when it was fined £400,000 for a data breach and also when it won a wooden spoon award for the Worst Customer Performance two years running.

"And she's on the board of the Jockey Club, which allowed the Cheltenham Festival to disastrously go ahead in March.

"Why are you trusting her with mine and my children's health?"

19/08/20. https://www.facebook.com/PeoplesMomentum/videos/307250104045266

Who is Dido Harding?

19/08/20. The level of corruption and cronyism in this Tory Government is now just beyond belief 👾👾👾👾

Just watching the Scottish News about coronavirus patients still suffering serious health problems 4 mths after "recovering".

Still believe that Johnson was close to death on a Wednesday but gave a Nationwide broadcast on Easter Sunday 4 DAYS later with no signs of a mild cold never mind a near fatal disease? 👾👾👾👾👾👾👾👾👾

Daily Mail

FREE INSIDE! PREMIER LEAGUE FIXTURES POSTER

PICTURE EXCLUSIVE

Exams fiasco, pupils let down — and not a word of sympathy from the PM. So what's the Mail found him doing instead?

BORIS CARRIES ON CAMPING!

21/08/20. Worldwide pandemic, a generation of children's futures at risk......Can this moronic cunt become any more of a moronic cunt? Unfortunately YES. 😡😡😡😡😡😡😡✂✂✂✂✂

Janey Godley - Loch Ness isn't in a swamp

https://www.youtube.com/watch?v=TopYYkVsUq8&list=UURvLN6EjLXIqteezXkpkU4A&index=62

21/08/20.

> For a while Houdini used trap doors in every act. ..... it was stage he was going through.
> I'm worried I might be an insomniac...but I'm going to sleep on it...
> I'm just back from a once in a lifetime trip.....never again...
> I got a knock back from that new Indian restaurant the other night.....didn't have a reservation...
> We have a beautiful little girl who we named after her mom, in fact Passive Aggressive Psycho turns 5 tomorrow.......
> I have a weird hobby .....I collect empty bottles, which sounds so much better than alcoholic.....
> Receiving oral sex from an ugly girl is like rock climbing..... you should never look down.....
> I went to a Karaoke Bar last night that didn't play any 70s music.... at first I was afraid, oh I was petrified.....

21/08/20. Dido Harding's husband part of an advisory board which called for PHE to be scrapped

It's becoming impossible to be surprised by the sheer level of corruption in this Government. INDEPENDENCE NOW ⬛⬛⬛⬛⬛⬛⬛⬛⬛⬛⬛⬛⬛⬛⬛⬛⬛⬛⬛⬛⬛⬛⬛⬛

Matt Carr
@MattCarr55

I'm 64. Lived under Thatcher. The Iraq catastrophe. 10 years of vicious 'austerity'. But this government is so brazenly malicious, ignorant, arrogant,corrupt, callous, dishonest, & incompetent that I still struggle to conceive how any country could have done this to itself.

People weren't able to drive during lockdown so I've written an algorithm to send speeding tickets to random drivers based on historic speeding records in their area.

23/08/20. I'm all for Nicola's speed and clarity of advice but there are some restrictions on bars and restaurants that are preventing them getting back to profitability. In Jeremiah's Tap Room to observe social distancing they need to operate a one way system which means when you go to the loo you then need to exit the pub, today in the rain and come back in to get to your table. No background music also seems harsh. It's like being in a bar on the Moon....just no atmosphere 🌚

24/08/20. While the Clowncil led by McVay not only repeat the same mistakes they make bigger ones. The tram extension down Leith was always an unnecessary waste of £millions but now with thousands of Edinburgh citizens working from home or with no jobs to commute to it will be an even bigger white elephant.

Now the question is.....do they have a sense of humour....or are the EGITS serious?

Letter printed in Edinburgh Evening News :-

After years of complaining, moaning and boring all my pals in the pub about the farcical. £1,000,000,000 vanity, white elephant destroying the most beautiful world heritage site, destroying small businesses all the way along a route that will never ever see a tram....I've came round to their way of thinking!
Yes, I have now formed Edinburgh Generating Integrated Transport Systems ....EGITS....we shall have regular monthly meetings at Harthill Service Station...its much more convenient than the city centre and parking is free.
I suggest our next project after completing the tram line from Edinburgh Airport to the Gogar roundabout should be to restore Prices St Gardens to their former glory....The Nor Loch!!! Yes we should flood the gardens and allow gondolas and pedillos to transport people the length of Princess St.
Of course we will need to enforce a strict one way system with no right turns or peddillos in the gondola lane with cameras to fine selfish peddilo-drivers and of course the whole loch will be patrolled by parking attendants on super charged jet skis to punish selfish peddilo-drivers by making them re-sit their peddilo-drivers test..
We would then of course demolish the eyesore of a castle and replace it with a more fitting building to our beautiful city. I would suggest a multi story glass tourist attraction selling traditional plastic kilts and "see you jimmie" ginger wigs and serving traditional Scottish Cuisine such as deep fried Mars Bars. Or we should at least adorn the Castle in similar outdoor displays of plastic kilts etc that are promoted outside most of our traditional shops in the High Street and Princess Street. This would also have the effect of diverting the attention of the

Planning Enforcement Officer before he notices that there are huge multiple poles the length of Princes Street and cables fixed to Category A Listed Buildings.
And for that Arthur Seat waste of space...that will be bulldozed to make way for a super stadium for the capitals most successful football team.......that's right Spartans.
IF you would like to support the EGITS campaign please send all donations to Tom King c/o Royal Edinburgh Hospital ....

Hitler on Edinburgh Trams Fiasco
http://www.youtube.com/watch?v=7yOqU4-zE5w

27/08/20. Bolingoli confirmed as Celtic Player of the Year after going further in Europe than the rest of his teammates put together......but the SFA award Celtic the 2020-21 SPL title as they think their title challenge will be adversely affected by their fans having to wash regularly.

Janey Godley - Rugby V football and the Curtain twitchers

https://www.youtube.com/watch?v=8ncfir6SG0E&list=UURvLN6EjLXIqteezXkpkU4A&index=61

28/08/20. Interesting wee article from Andrew Marr:

"We were up in Scotland following the loss of my father, a lifelong and keen reader of these pages. There, the difference in atmosphere over Covid is almost tangible compared with London. People are much more likely to be masked and much more cautious. They listen attentively to the First Minister, Nicola Sturgeon, and pride themselves on Scotland's lower death rates. The opinion polls confirm what general conversation suggests: that Scotland is likely to leave the United Kingdom before the end of this parliament. The SNP may be having feuds but they are self-confident, vigorous and optimistic. Unionism seems muffled and tired by comparison. But if independence happens, the end of GB is going to be a more traumatic moment for England than today's ministers seem able to grasp. It's going to feel much more significant than Brexit. The future of basic aspects of identity, like the Union Flag, the name of the country, its defence system, and the scope of its territory will be in question. Perhaps the PM grasps this. But his premiership may be defined by this and Unionists will need a far cleverer and more passionate politics than anything we have seen so far from Boris Johnson —

or indeed, Keir Starmer. Nothing in politics, as in life, is inevitable. But at the moment, the Scotland my father knew is slipping away."

What's interesting isn't so much the fact he saw what we all see everyday, but the use of the language "slipping away".

They have always viewed us as a colony.

Time tae boost, folks 👍

28/08/20. A guy can make £30 billion a day making door to door deliveries.....a guy can make £15 million a month for kicking a ball......a guy can get fined £1,000 for sleeping in a doorway because he is homeless ......we are a sick fucked up society😠😠😠😠😠😠😠😠😠😠😠

30/08/20 what we have witnessed during this crisis can leave no sane person in any doubt ......

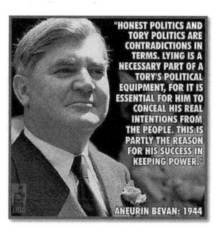

"HONEST POLITICS AND TORY POLITICS ARE CONTRADICTIONS IN TERMS. LYING IS A NECESSARY PART OF A TORY'S POLITICAL EQUIPMENT, FOR IT IS ESSENTIAL FOR HIM TO CONCEAL HIS REAL INTENTIONS FROM THE PEOPLE. THIS IS PARTLY THE REASON FOR HIS SUCCESS IN KEEPING POWER."

ANEURIN BEVAN: 1944

Janey Godley - House parties and David Icke and the lizards

https://www.youtube.com/watch?v=xqvl0wzNczc&list=UURvLN6EjLXIqteezXkpkU4A&index=5

Andrew Stroehlein ✔
@astroehlein

New BBC boss warns comedians not to joke about the government & its signature policy of brexit, and not to mock the Tories or Trump...

A chilling move to politicise entertainment shows and put them in the service of the ruling party.
telegraph.co.uk/news/2020/08/3...

The Telegraph

Exclusive: BBC's new boss threatens to axe Left-wing comedy shows

Tim Davie believes the BBC's comedy output is seen as too one-sided, and unfairly biased against the Tories, Donald Trump and Brexit

Phil Ferrie.
@blackdogday69

So,the city economy collapsing will be our fault now for not buying enough £6 sandwiches and £5 coffees...Nothing to do with billions wasted on useless PPE and giving contracts to 'mates' with no experience .....no,it's our fault for not buying coffee......Pricks.

18:27 · 28/08/2020 · Twitter Web App

693 Retweets and comments **1,835** Likes

We have a Government built on lies, sleaze, truth twisting & negligence. If the BBC won't step up to expose it I happily will.

01/09/10. We are rapidly heading for state led Dictatorship that will make North Korea seem like an enjoyable immigration destination from the UK. All led by the most corrupt, lying bunch of kunts ever to have power in the UK.

Breaking News....UK Prime Minister reported alive and well after unconfirmed reports that he had joined Thatcher in Hell. He's been spotted out horse riding...on Shergar accompanied by Dumbnut Cummings and Matt HandCock......The Three Horsemen Of The New Apocalypse leading us into the decline of western civilization. 🦍

ps. Have a nice day.......things can only get worse. ✖✖✖✖✖

Janey Godley - Glasgow lockdown

https://www.youtube.com/watch?v=_rfxTvqjYXQ&list=UURvLN6EjLXIqteezXkpkU4A&index=58

3/09/20. I know the Sturgeon/SNP haters love to nit pick and say Sturgeon is scaremongering to make Johnsons government look incompetent and stupid......that is impossible as David Copperfield could not make this government look more incompetent and stupid than they actually are......although maybe he is guilty of making the UK PM, in a time of world crisis, disappear? More likely his boss Dumbnut Cummings has barred him from opening his front door or his mouth.

Sturgeon has consistently explained in detail her reasoning rather than utter the "we are following the science" bullshit from down south.....and always first to admit any mistake. Have you heard one single Tory politician utter the word "sorry"? ♥✕✕✕✕✕✕✕✕✕✕

03/09/20. Boris left flailing as his linitations become clear for all to see

3/09/20. Boris Johnson's complete lack of shame has long been one of his defining narcissistic traits. His willingness to betray family, friends and colleagues for short-term personal gain is common knowledge. In much the same way, his lack of competence – his inability to grasp basic details – has also been priced in to the equation, as no one on the Tory benches much cared. It was just Boris being Boris. i.e. a moronic lying cunt. ●●●●●✕✕✕✕✕

A friend of mine, just started his own business in Afghanistan. He's making land-mines that look like prayer mats. It's doing well.

He says prophets are going through the roof!

Janey Godley - Ruth the baroness
https://www.youtube.com/watch?v=I1UFQoQJCmo&list=UURvLN6EjLXlqteezXkpkU4A&index=

_53_

5/09/11. Boris Johnson has appointed Tony Abbott as an official UK trade adviser, defying widespread condemnation of the former Australian prime minister's record of misogyny and homophobia and his views on the climate emergency.

5/09/20. Ex Australian PM Tony Abbot is being appointed to advise post Brexit UK on world trade. Tony Abbott is a misogynist, homophobe & recently said the elderly should have been allowed to die from Covid.

Compare Handcock's response to Nicola Sturgeon's and it sums up the difference between Tory and Scottish morals.

Hancock - "As the former Prime Minister of Australia, Mr Abbott obviously has a huge amount of experience,"

Burley asked: "Even if he is a homophobic misogynist?"

"He is also an expert in trade," replied Mr Hancock.

Nicola Sturgeon - "Tony Abbott is a misogynist, sexist & climate change denier... his comments about letting the elderly die are a disgrace ......with his morals he should not be an Ambassador to the UK or any other country"

No one is too morally corrupt to represent a Tory Government. 😡😡😡😡😡✖✖✖✖

5/09/10. NO. We are paying to keep them in relative luxury for the rest of their lives. Lethal injection is the only option when someone is caught literally red handed slaughtering an innocent young man.

"AFTER GOD MADE ME, HE HAD SOME SKIN, GIBLETS AND SHIT LEFT OVER AND HE THREW THIS CNUT TOGETHER"

5/09/20.   Boris Johnson...out of his depth on a wet pavement...

Dam missed my train Oh well...😎 Shit.. missed another train. . Fuck it...."excuse me waitress"

A Dublin man sees a sign outside a Kerry farmhouse:
'Talking Dog for Sale'....He rings the bell; the owner appears and tells him the dog can be viewed in the back garden.
The man sees a very nice looking Black Labrador Retriever sitting there.
"Do you really talk?" He asks the dog.
"Yes!" The Labrador replies.
After recovering from the shock of hearing the dog talk, the man asks, "So, tell me your story!"
The Labrador looks up and says, "Well, I discovered that I could talk when I was pretty young. I wanted to help the government, so I joined the Garda.
"In no time at all they had me jetting from country to country, sitting in rooms with spies and world drug lords, because no one imagined that a dog would be eavesdropping.
I was one of their most valuable spies for eight years, But the jetting around really tired me out, and I knew I wasn't getting any younger so I decided to settle down. I signed up for a job at Dublin airport to do some undercover security work, wandering near suspicious characters and listening in. I uncovered some incredible dealings and was awarded several medals. I got married, had a few puppies, and now I've just retired!"
The man is amazed. He goes back into the house and asks the Kerryman how much he wants for the dog.
"Ten quid!" The owner says.
"£10? But this dog is absolutely amazing! Why on earth are you selling him so cheaply?"
"Because he's a lying cunt. He's never been out of the garden!"

Peter Stefanovic
@PeterStefanovi2

It will come as no surprise to anyone that a man twice sacked for lying, who misled the Queen & unlawfully suspended Parliament, who sacked 20 of his MP's for disagreeing with him & put lives at risk to keep his adviser in a job would also renege on the UK's legal obligations

07:31 · 9/7/20 · Twitter for iPhone

07/09/20.   The cunt should be in jail 😡😡😡

08/09/20 Johnson's Conservative Party have been lambasted after making a *"shameful u-turn"* to vote down an amendment to put into law the fire safety recommendations made during phase one of the official Grenfell Inquiry. Disgusting 😠😠😠😠😠😠😠

Janey Godley - Covid ni ni nineteen
https://www.youtube.com/watch?v=FNUe5zO7xo0&list=UURvLN6EjLXlqteezXkpkU4A&index=

<u>51</u>

08/09/20 "Brexit deal never made sense" says man who negotiated it, signed it, prevented MPs from scrutinising it, campaigned for it and won a general election on the back of it.

This lying cunt is simply devoid of feeling shame. 😠😠😠😠😠😠

09/09/20. **What I hope we will see.**   **The only image that would have given me more pleasure....**

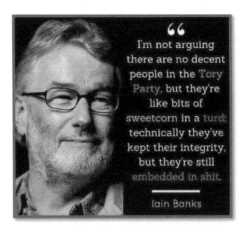

I'm not arguing there are no decent people in the Tory Party, but they're like bits of sweetcorn in a turd: technically they've kept their integrity, but they're still embedded in shit.

Iain Banks

09/09/20. Nicola Sturgeon.

"The Internal Market Bill that the U.K. government will publish today is a full frontal assault on devolution. And to the usual "but the SNP would say that" voices, read the Welsh Government view below, rightly referring to the Bill 'stealing' powers from the devolved governments.

At forthcoming Scottish Parliament elections, the SNP will make case for independence. And more and more this is not about independence vs the status quo of devolution. It's about independence as the only way to protect the Scottish Parliament from being undermined and its powers eroded.

And added to all of the above, this is a Bill that, by the government's own admission, breaks international law. This UK gov is the most reckless (& to make it worse, incompetently so) and unprincipled in my lifetime. Scotland can do better and we will have that choice".

09/09/20. If the level of lies and corruption from this Tory government was not already beyond belief they now openly admit they are going to break International Law on Brexit. 😡😡😡 But let's be clear you are now expected not to break government guidelines ....such as if you go outdoors please stay indoors, only drive if it's an emergency or if to test your eyesight, only meet with elderly parents if the purpose is to kill them and get them off benefits, only meet in groups of six if it's to get a taxi to a rave, only meet in groups of 1,000 if it's to go and watch cricket, wear a mask at all times except when housebreaking or shoplifting, wash your fucking hands if you shake hands with a Tory. Remember these measures must be strictly adhered to with the only exceptions being if you are a lying, cheating Tory cunt.....because obviously the laws of the land only apply to the poor plebs....not millionaire cunts that think they are above the law.

Are You Yes Yet.........or just stupid? 💋✖✖✖✖✖✖✖✖✖

Janey Godley - We did warn you all

https://www.youtube.com/watch?v=goLro45IVt4&list=UURvLN6EjLXIqteezXkpkU4A&index=4

9

09/09/20. Matt Hancock 'comfortable' with government breaking international law in 'limited and specific way'

Is punching the fuck out of any Tory MP in a 'limited and specific way' allowed? Asking for a friend.

Janey Godley - No more daily briefings on BBC

https://www.youtube.com/watch?v=21VKKG--

DBo&list=UURvLN6EjLXIqteezXkpkU4A&index=48

10/09/20. BA boss Willie Walsh gets £883k annual bonus as thousands of workers axed.

How the fuck does anyone justify any bonus for failing at their job?

The current situation is obviously not his fault but he has been paid £33,000,000 in 9 years FFS. He is another Tory cunt for accepting a bonus while throwing loyal employees on the scrapheap.

When the government says you can have up to six people in your garden.

10/09/20. Can anyone clarify please. If the first six are deid.....can yi have another six live ones? Asking for a friend. 😎✖️

IMAGINE NO RELIGION.

11/09/20.   Never Forget.......who was responsible....? 😎

How the fuck during the biggest crisis since World War Two did we end up with two imbeciles in charge of the US and UK.

"They say that people on benefits aren't contributing to society but if anything they're contributing the most.

You think their £56 a week is going into an offshore account or straight into a high yield ISA? No it's going straight back into the economy because they can't afford to save it. That money is being used to buy food, pay bills.

Even if all they did was drink and smoke they'd still be paying more UK tax individually last year than the whole of Amazon."

We must recognize "the news" is no longer "news", but propaganda to change our way of thinking.

12/09/20. Tommy Tank, Eric The Hun, Big Bawbag and Billy The Buddha having a quiet evening of reflection on living through a world pandemic.....but getting pished and feeling the love. 🍺

13/09/20. Have you noticed these Romanian street beggars placed along Princes Street by their warlords are now increasing attractive young women? The theory will be drunk or just lecherous guys will give them money before giving to a bearded auld jackey wie a matted mutt. I was passing one when I took the time to stop and read the card she was holding......"I'm homeless, I have 2 children, 3 dogs and 4 cats and my husband is a cunt who takes all my money and refuses to look for work. I have never been able to learn English and have no money and I am desperate......the new iPhone comes out next week and I need an upgrade...please help?" I looked at her and thought....if you have never learned English you could get a job as a sign writer ya fucker... Anyway I did my elephant impersonation and pulled my pockets inside out and shrugged "Sorry no cash" she looked up, smiled.......and reached under her blanket and whipped out a contactless card machine! WTF.....I "said what's your name?" "Ivana Sukyakokov" Why did you not say that earlier.....get yer card machine and meet up the lane. 💋✂

13/09/20. WE NEED TO TAKE BACK CONTROL

We need to take back control of our agriculture. We need to take back control of our waters and our fishing stock. We need to be able to control our own borders and decide who crosses them. We need to take back control of our Laws and our political decisions. We need to be able to form trade agreements with other nations to suit our own needs.

It is not right that people we do not elect sit in another parliament in another country and make laws affecting our everyday lives. It is not right that another parliament in another country dictates how and when we spend much of our own income.

There is no country in the world that should be forced to stay in a union against its will. We want to be able to decide our own future on our own terms.

You may think those statements are yet more tired old rhetoric from the Nasty Nationalists about why they want independence for Scotland from the rest of the United Kingdom and in particular Westminster.

They are, in fact, arguments made by Brexiteers to justify why they wanted independence for the United Kingdom from the European Union and in particular Brussels.

However, with a few minor adjustments such as changing the United Kingdom to Scotland and Brussels to Westminster they make a perfect case for Scottish independence.

Thanks guys because every word you uttered to make the case for the United Kingdom leaving the European Union demonstrates exactly why Scotland should leave the United Kingdom.

God I love this country

14/09/20. You could not make this shit up. 📱

A completely corrupt UK government led by a PM that has been sacked for lying from every job he's held, illegally shut down parliament, lied to the Queen, won a GE by lies, deceit and corruption based on lying to the nation that he had signed an "oven ready" Brexit deal, now prepared to break international law because the agreement he signed will lead to a Customs Border with Ireland which he lied to the nation about. Taking orders from a man that took his family for a car journey to test his eyesight after breaking his own rules regarding not driving more than 50 miles from home. Who boasted about shaking hands with hospital patients, who allowed 250,000 people to attend a horse racing event when Italy and Spain were already going into total lockdown.

A ferry company with no ships awarded a £40 million ferry contract.

£Billions paid to almost non existing companies to provide PPE that was never delivered. Contact tracers paid £450 pw without contacting a single person.

This is a corruptly elected UK PM who caused thousands of unnecessary deaths by adopting Herd Immunity Strategy at the start of the crisis.

This is a corruptly elected UK PM who almost certainly lied to the world that he was near to death from coronavirus

Why? Because they are the "I'm alright Jack just keep your hands of my stack" type who do not care about a fairer caring society where hard working individuals can prosper without turning their backs on the poor, sick and disabled members of our SOCIETY. 💘⬛⬛⬛⬛⬛⬛⬛⬛⬛⬛⬛⬛⬛⬛⬛

14/09/20. **Labour will back new Brexit legislation if PM addresses concerns, says Starmer**

WTF. The Labour leader, a lawyer supporting a Tory Government breaking International Law? The UK is fucked. Would the last person to leave this fucked up Union switch off the lights please? 💘⬛

14/09/20. **Grouse Shooting And Hunting Exempt From Johnson's 'Rule Of Six' Covid Curbs**

FFS....I suppose Morris Dancing will also be exempt 😊📱 sad thing is my mate Morris can't fuckin dance in the first place 😊

15/09/20. Nicola Sturgeon has said Scots should not be "spying on your neighbours" following a UK Government minister calling on people in England to ring the police if they are concerned the new rules are being breached. 💘⬛⬛⬛⬛⬛⬛⬛⬛⬛⬛⬛

So shop thy neighbour - lawbreaking advice from the Law breaking UK Government. 📱📱📱📱

15/09/20. Peers begged for 'hardship fund' after daily allowance was cut to £162

These cunts simply have no shame......Rooth The Mooth and Mony Michele probably at the front of the queue 😡😡😡😡😡❌❌❌❌❌

15/09/20. Just had an MOT, heart fine, bloods good, no sign of diabetes or prostate cancer and the Doc says my liver will last a lifetime......if I die by tea time Tuesday 😊

Janey Godley - Princess Anne Tupperware party
https://www.youtube.com/watch?v=5ipVkR-Oka0&list=UURvLN6EjLXIqteezXkpkU4A&index=45

15/09/20. Coronavirus: Shooting parties exempt from 'rule of six'

Now if someone shoots the entire UK Cabinet, who are clearly a danger to life....is that just breaking the law in "a measured and acceptable way?" Just asking on behalf of the entire fuckin country 😵😵😵

16/09/20. President Trump at California wildfire briefing: "It'll start getting cooler. You just watch"

California Secretary for Natural Resources Wade Crowfoot: "I wish science agreed with you."

Trump: "Well, I don't think science knows, actually"

Can this moronic cunt get any more moronic? Unfortunately YES 😵😵😵

16/09/20. Hate to do this about my favourite Chinese restaurant in Edinburgh, but feel you deserve to know. 😵
** Be aware **
I ordered a takeaway (I won't name them yet) I went to pick it up and as I as driving home, heard the bags rustling and moving!!!
I thought what in the world is that? Has something got in the bag? I thought I could see a little pair of eyes peering out
I was driving so I leaned forward, picked up the bag, put it on the passenger seat and there it was again, more rustling and little eyes looking out behind the prawn crackers,
I thought it's got to be a rat or a mouse or something, so I carefully pulled the bag down ...
And there it was ...
... A Peeking Duck
😵😵😵 so don't get yer carry oot fi Wan Kin Palace

Janey Godley - 17 September 2020
https://www.youtube.com/watch?v=nbAIhSYBN2Y&list=UURvLN6EjLXIqteezXkpkU4A&index=

43

18/09/2020. Boris Johnson's Brexit plan will break the UK union

Wouldn't it be justice if we gain Independence because of this moronic lying cunt breaking International Law? Karma. 😎

David Schneider
@davidschneider

In this week's Satire Is Dead, man who spent £50m on ferry company with no ferries gets £100k job as adviser to ports.

BBC NEWS
Grayling to advise ports operator in £100,000 role

18/09/20 Not really a surprise ...the Tory cunts made a moronic serial liar cheat and lawbreaker UK PM......Harold Shipman Chief Medical Officer, Jimmy Saville Minister for Childcare and Fred West Minister for Home Improvements. 😡😡😡😡😡✂️✂️✂️

19/09/20. More blatant Tory corruption. Does anyone buy this for one single, solitary moment? This is called 'destroying evidence' and should be prosecuted to the full extent of the law

There is simply nothing these cunts will not stoop to for their own self interests. If you are a Tory supporter just hang your head in shame........apologies....if you are a Tory supporter just hang yourself......please.

19/09/20. Hundreds of Scots miners who received criminal convictions during the bitter strike of the 80s are set to be pardoned.

WOW. this will be good news for all the guys in their 70's and 80's who can now apply for work after being on a Tory blacklist for nearly 40 years.....the ones that passed away with a stain on their character can now R.I.P.

https://www.dailyrecord.co.uk/news/politics/hundreds-scots-miners-convicted-during-22707625

20/09/20. A company that donated more than £400,000 to the Conservative Party has received a £93.8 million Government contract for the supply of respirator face masks.

A spokesman for the company "Last Gasp Masks", Dick Turpin said "we will have a world beating mask that will stop the sick and elderly breathing within minutes"

There are now rogue African Dictators complaining the UK has the most corrupt Government in the world. 😵😵🏴🏴

https://bylinetimes.com/2020/09/16/company-conservative-donations-government-ppe-procurement-deal/

20/09/20. So is the type of person that will breach covid rules enough to end up with a£10,000 fine going to pay it? What then jail? How about a retrospective £1,000,000 fine for Dumbnut Cummings for testing his eyes with a family drive? How about a retrospective £1,000,000 fine for the cunt handing out £100,000,000 PPE contracts to their buddies with no tender process or evidence of actually manufacturing PPE? How about a £10,000,000 fine for the stupid cunt that signed an "oven ready" Brexit deal and refuses to honour his promise of dying in a ditch? How about a £100,000,000 fine for the cunt that recommends the UK government breaking international law? 💣✖✖✖✖✖✖✖✖

21/09/20. You can blow out a candle but you can't blow out a fire. That fire is now Scottish Independence from one of the world's most corrupt governments....the Tory UK Government.

21/09/20. If Covid only comes out at 10 pm why don't we all go to the pub at 8 am?

and another thing....if the bastard only kills if you play loud music and turn the TV volume up....why are we safer at home?.....lets all go to the pub ....nae loud music or tv!!!

21/09/20. Number 10 denies Boris Johnson 'spent long weekend in Italy' this month.

Johnston yet to deny he went to Italy.....so what? He denies he is a law breaking, lying, cheating cunt....but everyone knows he is.

21/09/20. Ok let's start with the easy ones to solve this world crisis. 1) Sack the non elected Dumnut Cummings who is the one advising the so called PM and then ignoring his own advice and charge him with putting lives at risk. 2) Raise a vote of no confidence in the UK government and force Johnson resignation 3) Implement emergency legislation to form a coalition of all UK political parties. 4) Form a committee of non political scientific advisers to the coalition. 5) Prosecute all Ministers that have awarded £Billions to almost non existent PPE manufacturers. 6) Divert the available £Billions to a world beating test and trace system and an antidote 7) Request a legal enquiry into the UK Governments handling of the crisis with jail sentences for any minister found guilty of lying to or misleading the uk citizens. 8) Replace the Queen with St Nicola. 9) Reverse the Religious Bigotry influenced decision of the SFA to award the SPL Title to Sceptic and relegate The Jam Tarts. 10) Relegate any SPL team whose director's vote against 9). OK world crisis solved. Now lets move on to how to make your wife happy in bed...1) Leave home...2) Give her my phone number

23/09/20. Is there method in the madness? Like the majority I don't have a fucking clue! Some of the "rules" and contradictions appear ludicrous ....can't visit other households but can go to the pub? no background music, no volume on the TV etc etc. But one thing I do know is that I don't want to see mass graves, ICU wards overflowing, mortuaries overflowing and NHS front line staff dying trying to save others. These are the things we witnessed only a few months ago and risk seeing again with even worse consequences in a second wave. Is it the worst thing in the world to wear a face mask? Phone or even zoom relatives? Be out the pub by 10 pm? It's the pub hours I grew up with. The rules and contradictions are tough to accept but in most cases an inconvenience rather than a threat to lives ......that we could be faced with for years if we don't eradicate/control this virus.

Direct your anger and frustration at the individuals that not only caused unnecessary deaths but profited from them......Cummings/Johnson's Tory Government.

Direct action/protest marches are not acceptable but use social media against them the same way they have used social media against us.

Don't just like or dislike posts.....use your social media voice....express yourself. Of course it may be futile...but maybe not?

In pre Covid times posting pictures of your dinner, your cat, your country walk were fabulous.......our world has changed. Of course they are still images we all want to see and I'm as guilty by posting pics of having a beer outside my locals......but they are far outnumbered by venting my anger at the social inequality and corrupt establishment we need to change.

Vent your anger and frustrations at the vile corrupt UK establishment ......not the people trying to save lives. Luv n Peace and Stay Safe.

Janey Godley - That's it baws on the dyke

https://www.youtube.com/watch?v=1_3V9Tzz4Co&list=UURvLN6EjLXIqteezXkpkU4A&index=39

At this point I'd feel safer if the Coronavirus held a press conference telling us how it was going to protect us from the Government

23/09/20. FFS...greetin pusses..."why can I go to the pub but I can't visit my 90 yr old Gran?" By all means go and visit your Gran.....if you don't care whether she makes 91.

The bars/restaurants that I frequent even although they know me personally I still need to give my contact details or scan their app at the door, some also take temperature, masks must be worn unless seated, tables are 2m apart, disinfected before a new customer can be seated, all contact points and toilets are cleaned every hour. Which one of these do you do if you go to visit family? Probably the first thing you do is hug them without a second thought for where you have been or the strangers you may have been in close contact with. And for the dicks that complain more people die from cancer every day......you can't fuckin infect your Gran with cancer. ●Stay Strong and Stay Safe. ♥✖✖✖✖✖✖✖✖✖

24/09/20. "The United Kingdom has fallen. There has been a right wing coup in this country... . And nobody noticed. We did not notice because it was years in the making. We did not notice because when it came, it came in a blonde wig and a mask of buffoonery. We did not notice because it lied to us and hid its true intent. We did not notice because the foreign manipulation was hidden from us and continues to be hidden from us. We did not notice, because the lies when they were discovered were hidden by more lies, until lack of truth became normal and acceptable. We didn't notice because it appealed to our basest nature. It cried racist, it cried xenophobe, it falsified a threat to our way of life and blamed others. We did not notice because we accepted all the promises and lies and now we cannot admit to our gullibility.

Make no mistake it has been moving steadily and stealthily. Have you not noticed how Parliament has been emasculated and how decisions are now taken by a few in a closed room? Have you noticed how the judiciary is being sidelined? Have you noticed how the media are controlled & access to news is restricted? The BBC merely mouths faceless government sources and the papers howl racist xenophobic and government-fed lies?

Have you noticed how the police, under cover of COVID, are being encouraged gradually to interfere more and more in our lives? Have you noticed how we are being encouraged to report 'unsocial behavior' in our neighbor's? Have you noticed how the impartial Civil Service is being packed with yes men and government cronies? Committee after committee is rigged with government-friendly sympathisers.

Even now a review of the Armed Services is underway. Have you noticed how every means of objection or complaint is being stealthily closed? Have you noticed the intention to lower food standards, animal & environmental standards and abandon the guarantees of our basic human rights? Have you noticed how measures trumpeted as keeping foreigners out, actually make it harder for US to leave? Finally have you noticed how the government is engineering circumstances under which everyone's lives will be so much harder and under which we will have so much more to worry about than complain about our government?

Meanwhile the rape and asset- stripping of the country has already begun, with million-pound contracts awarded to cronies with no apparent expertise, siphoning money from the public purse to the private pocket and delivering nothing.

It may already be too late but surely the time has come to cry enough! To stand up against the lies, the manipulation, the takeover of our Society. This government does not govern for the people; this government is governing for itself. It has become an enemy of the people, its actions are treasonous. Surely it is time to demand better, time to TAKE BACK CONTROL."

26/09/20. Maybe she's just full? It's been a long lockdown 😴

Johnson's "world beating" test and trace "NHS=Serco" app cannot work if you have had an NHS test. Fucking unbelievable. The most corrupt government the UK has even known.

26/09/20. Councillors to discuss ambitious plans to extend Edinburgh Trams to Fife.

Are these arsehole Clowncillers serious?

Will it be a new bridge? Will it be a tunnel? Will it be amphibious? Will they knock down the Forth Rail Bridge to make way for it?

These areholes are being paid salaries to waste time on their fantasies then say they need to make redundancies and close public toilets due to budget deficit. 😂😂😂😂😂

https://www.google.com/search?q=Councillors+to+discuss+ambitious+plans+to+extend+Edinburgh+Trams+to+Fife.&rlz=1C1NHXL_enGB836GB836&oq=Councillors+to+discuss+ambitious+plans+to+extend+Edinburgh+Trams+to+Fife.&aqs=chrome..69i57.1531j0j15&sourceid=chrome&ie=UTF-8

Things money can't buy:
1. Manners
2. Morals
3. Respect
4. Character
5. Common sense
6. Trust
7. Patience
8. Class
9. Integrity
10. Love

If you want proof just look at the £Millionaire Tory's. 😡✕✕✕✕✕

29/09/20. Several Edinburgh taxi drivers have been charged with breaching their licence. Police in the Capital have reported that several taxis were illegally ranking at the widened pavement on Princes Street contrary to the terms of their licence.

The Clowncil install measures to assist the non existent visitors to the cancelled festivals they then widen the pavements even further and not only reduce the road width they remove the taxi ranks forcing the decimated taxi trade to cruise the streets using fuel looking for non existent fares....or the police charge them for ranking in frustration to try and save fuel. Why do Adam McVey and Lesley McInnes still have jobs and salaries? 😡😡😡😡😡😡😡

28/09/20. **Fourth firm with links to Dominic Cummings awarded £640,000 in government work without an open tender process**

Looks like the cunt's gone totally blind .... to Tory corruption 😡😡😡😡

https://www.theneweuropean.co.uk/brexit-news/ex-vote-leave-campaign-director-wins-covid-gov-work-the-91030

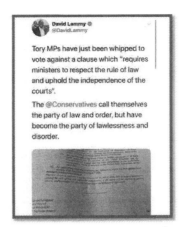

30/09/20. This on the same day the same cunts made singing and dancing illegal? George Orwell will be turning in his grave and saying "don't be so fucking ridiculous" ⚫⚫⚫⚫⚫⚫⚫

01/10/20. Sober October, anyone know what morning in October it is? 👓✖

This should be interesting. ▨▨▨▨▨▨▨▨▨

1/10/20. **Stanley Johnson says he doesn't fully understand the rules after he is caught shopping without a mask**

The shit that comes out these cunts is like diarrhea......it runs in their genes....⚫⚫⚫▨▨▨▨▨▨▨▨

1/10/20.   Is it a surprise that a dick used his dick to produce a dick?

2/10/20.Donald Trump Tests Positive for Covid-19 Along With First Lady Melania.

Tweet from Johnson to Trump "remember what I told you......stay out of sight for a couple weeks, reappear on the White House Steps and tell the Nation you were close to death and only survived because you had Medical Insurance .....remember to say sorry to the millions that cant afford it though....it's a winner Buddy the plebs will fall for it. Tell them how you do it best....you know...."the doctors said no one has ever been better at being close to death as me shite" .....it's a vote winner Don mate...if a stupid, lying cunt like me can pull it off so can you ....you're a much bigger, lying cunt that me"

Janey Godley - Margaret a Covid on a train
https://www.youtube.com/watch?v=y65bMWWKItg&list=UURvLN6EjLXIqteezXkpkU4A&index=34

Janey Godley – Margaret Covid
https://www.youtube.com/watch?v=v1QOhNWG0Gs&list=UURvLN6EjLXIqteezXkpkU4A&index=35

2/10/20 A kick right in the baws to Johnston but he's too moronic to realise it. St Nicola shows her strength in leadership with honesty and sadness. 👓

Janey Godley - 2 October 2020

https://www.youtube.com/watch?v=38rNUBuvz_8&list=UURvLN6EjLXIqteezXkpkU4A&index= 33

3/10/20. Fucking brilliant fb...."false information found in your post" do you cunts not watch the News or the daily briefings by Johnson, Handcock, Rabb and Non Priti Patel? 😂😂😂😂😂😂

3/10/20. Nicola Sturgeon says Matt Hancock tried to limit Scotland's coronavirus testing
Are You Yes Yet? ✖✖✖✖✖✖✖✖✖✖✖✖✖✖

https://www.thenational.scot/news/18719596.nicola-sturgeon-says-matt-hancock-tried-limit-scotlands-coronavirus-testing/

3/10/20. FFS the Doctors are now contradicting White House statements and Trumps own timeline of when he tested positive............US following the Johnson UK lead.....lie and cover up....I smell shite 💩💩💩💩

4/10/20

So did some fucker switch off the oven and we now have a microwave oven ready meal.....for one? 😂😂😂😂

4/10/20 Hancock Hanging Himself with False Positives

"The definition of insanity is doing the same thing over and over again and expecting different results."

Do these cunts think that we are suddenly going to believe them? They are insane. 😡😡😡😡😡✖✖✖✖

https://www.youtube.com/watch?v=5Qdm9CDQguM&feature=youtu.be&fbclid=IwAR32y5UDDZObVkwz6CKeMO7_Zf-tjlJIRXsl-SMrrac-vvTQ_uBiz0exTfY

"We thought we were to bring something for your coughing" 😄

Did I miss the Government announcement that pavements should be widened for social distancing? Or did Edinburgh Clowncil just decide tens of thousands of cones all over the city was not an expensive enough option so they have now gone for a more expensive option? Ok I suppose but they are being installed where there are almost no pedestrians 🌚

6/10/20 Who Is Dido Harding?

https://www.facebook.com/watch/?v=307250104045266

Don't forget Dildo Hardon was Chair Person of the Jockey Club when Cheltenham was given the go ahead while Spain and Italy were going into lockdown. 🌚

6/10/20. Covid: 16,000 coronavirus cases missed in daily figures after IT error
What should we expect? Johnson said in April "we will have a world beating test and trace app" Like most people I thought we would turn to the experts....but no £billions handed over to New Co Private Testicles and Trace.......not because of their expertise....but because Cummings, Whitey and other Boris Bum chums had shares in them. I hate to say it but do you think an Apple/Google/FB collaboration would have saved lives? They kinda know what they are doing when it comes to tracking our every fucking thought and movements....... Yeah of course these would have made huge profits but this is down to saving fucking lives and I kinda think they know what they are doing.....I doubt if their app would say "If you are worried about losing your eyesight immediately put the wife and kids in the car and go for a test drive" 🌀🌀🌀🌀🌀🌀🌀✄

6/10/20. What happened to big fines for serial offenders? from Cummings to this arrogant arse actually smiling at the camera they are a disgusting inbred bunch of selfish cunts. ARE YOU YES YET? ✄✄✄✄✄✄✄✄✄✄✄✄✄

7/10/20. I hope St Nicola does not impose blanket restrictions that prevent people returning to some form of normality in their personal and business lives. I think the vast majority of people understand why restrictions are required when we see rates of infection that are higher than in March but thankfully the hospital admissions and death rate are very, very low compared to March/April.

Some people complained "Oh I can go the pub but I can't see my granny in her house". The fact is that your granny was probably safer in the pub conforming to the guidelines than she was in her house being cuddled and kissed by you after returning from the supermarket on the bus. However, I doubt anyone can see how 10pm curfews and no background music in a bar/restaurant save lives.

It is obvious that allowing students to return to campus and halls of residence was a huge mistake. I completely understand the younger group can spread the virus to older or more vulnerable groups and the spread needs to be controlled but how many deaths have there been in fit, healthy 18 - 24 yr olds?

Surely this type of data can be analysed to bring in specific guidelines rather than apply guidelines to the whole population that is only going to protect 1%?

I am not advocating Herd Immunity as that requires a vaccine but we need to stop issuing guidelines that seem random, ill thought through to the majority or they will not be adhered to. The public also need to see Cummings, Ferrier and especially Johnson Snr prosecuted.

Anyway what the worst that can happen? You get coronavirus and nearly die? Don't worry you will be fit and healthy again in 4 days....just ask Johnson. Stay Safe and Sensible and don't follow your leader....unless it's St Nicola 😊✖✖✖✖✖✖✖✖✖✖

BREAKING
Tories announce groundbreaking new technology for the Track and Trace app

Diane Abbott....."where are the instructions please?" 😊

7/10/20 Not exactly what I hoped from St Nicola but as usual she was very clear and able to explain exactly why the measures were being taken. So no beer in pub for 16 days. 😔 even Rooth The Mooth struggled to criticize .....but she tried. 😠

Janey Godley - October
https://www.youtube.com/watch?v=5l9fjcx0rqU&list=UURvLN6EjLXIqteezXkpkU4A&index=29

07/10/20. Boris Johnson to unveil plan to power all UK homes with wind by 2030

Yep the cunt is going to come and shout and fart through every letter box in the UK.

https://www.theguardian.com/politics/2020/oct/05/boris-johnson-to-unveil-plan-to-power-all-uk-homes-with-wind-by-2030

Janey Godley - No more daily briefings on BBC

https://www.youtube.com/watch?v=21VKKG--

DBo&list=UURvLN6EjLXIqteezXkpkU4A&index=48

08/10/20. Plenty petty negative comments about Sturgeons new limited 16 day lockdown. The comments were generally "She's lost the plot" "it's nonsense" "She's an idiot" or much worse personal insults but with no debate or offers of an alternative. If you were faced with this graph below and had to make her decision what would you do? Take action to try and avoid a horrendous increase in infection rates leading to deaths or sit back and do nothing?

Doing nothing could have resulted in going back to March death rates or higher. The alternative is a complete lockdown. Luv n Peace stay safe and see you in 16 DAYS......not 16 weeks....not 16 months......which it could easily be if the rate of infection is not slowed.
♥✕✕✕✕✕✕✕✕✕

Janey Godley - Big bad Nicola

https://www.youtube.com/watch?v=P2_Zk4Lkj8k&list=UURvLN6EjLXIqteezXkpkU4A&index=26

08/10/20

A good read my Lady friends........if I have any? 💋✂

MEN ARE JUST HAPPY PEOPLE

This needs no explanation - and is a fun read, no matter your gender.

Men Are Just Happier People!

What do you expect from such simple creatures? Your last name stays put. The garage is all yours. Wedding plans take care of themselves. Chocolate is just another snack. You can never be pregnant. You can wear a white T-shirt to a water park. You can wear NO shirt to a water park.

Car mechanics tell you the truth. The world is your urinal. You never have to drive to another gas station restroom because this one is just too icky. You don't have to stop and think of which way to turn a nut on a bolt. Wrinkles add character. Wedding dress - $5,000. Tux rental - $100. People never stare at your chest when you're talking to them. New shoes don't cut, blister, or mangle your feet. One mood all the time. Phone conversations are over in 30 seconds flat. You know stuff about tanks.

A five-day vacation requires only one suitcase. You can open all your own jars. You get extra credit for the slightest act of thoughtfulness. If someone forgets to invite you, he or she can still be your friend. Your underwear is $8.95 for a three-pack. Two pairs of shoes are more than enough. You almost never have strap problems in public. You are unable to see wrinkles in your clothes. Everything on your face stays its original colour. The same hairstyle lasts for years, maybe decades. You only have to shave your face and neck.

You can play with toys all your life. One wallet and one pair of shoes - one colour for all seasons. You can wear shorts no matter how your legs look. You can 'do' your nails with a pocket knife. You have freedom of choice concerning growing a moustache... You can do Christmas shopping for 25 relatives on December 24 in 25 minutes.

No wonder men are happier!

NICKNAMES

• If Laura, Kate and Sarah go out for lunch, they will call each other Laura, Kate and Sarah.

• If Mike, Dave and John go out, they will affectionately refer to each other as Fat Boy, Bubba and Wildman.

EATING OUT

• When the bill arrives, Mike, Dave and John will each throw in $20, even though it's only for $32.50. None of them will have anything smaller and none will actually admit they want change back.

When the girls get their bill, outcome the pocket calculators.

MONEY

- A man will pay $2 for a $1 item he needs.

- A woman will pay $1 for a $2 item that she doesn't need but it's on sale.

BATHROOMS

- A man has six items in his bathroom: toothbrush, toothpaste, shaving cream, razor, a bar of soap, and a towel.

- The average number of items in the typical woman's bathroom is 337. A man would not be able to identify more than 20 of these items.

ARGUMENTS

- A woman has the last word in any argument.

- Anything a man says after that is the beginning of a new argument.

FUTURE

- A woman worries about the future until she gets a husband.

- A man never worries about the future until he gets a wife.

MARRIAGE

- A woman marries a man expecting he will change, but he doesn't.

- A man marries a woman expecting that she won't change, but she does.

DRESSING UP

- A woman will dress up to go shopping, water the plants, empty the trash, answer the phone, read a book, and get the mail.

- A man will dress up for weddings and funerals.

NATURAL

- Men wake up as good-looking as they went to bed.

- Women somehow deteriorate during the night.

OFFSPRING

- Ah, children. A woman knows all about her children. She knows about dentist appointments and romances, best friends, favourite foods, secret fears and hopes and dreams.

- A man is vaguely aware of some short people living in the house.

THOUGHT FOR THE DAY

A married man should forget his mistakes. There's no use in two people remembering the same thing!

So, send this to the women who have a sense of humour .... and to the men who will enjoy reading.

Janey Godley - Jaffa day

https://www.youtube.com/watch?v=fXnbrAGJdGo&list=UURvLN6EjLXIqteezXkpkU4A&index=27

BREAKING NEWS ...

John Travolta was hospitalized for suspected COVID-19, but doctors now confirm that it was only Saturday Night Fever, and they assure everyone that he is Staying Alive.

Apparently, he had chills that were multiplying.

Janey Godley - Blackpool

https://www.youtube.com/watch?v=7KAR60seIE8&list=UURvLN6EjLXIqteezXkpkU4A&index=25

9/10/20 New restrictions to reduce the spread of Covid come into force today and tomorrow.

Nicola Sturgeon said "I really do know this is tough. But this is about saving lives and keeping each other as safe and well as we possibly can."

A few recent press headlines.

Nicola Sturgeon crowned 'Politician of the Year'. 22 November 2019.

Nicola Sturgeon voted 'most impressive politician' during Covid-19.

Boris Johnson: Officially the most appalling PM that could have been plucked from a pool of 66million imperfect humans

'Boris Johnson is a shameless pathological liar who will let you down'.

Boris Johnson set to shut pubs and restaurants in northern England in new local lockdown. The move comes just hours after First Minister Nicola Sturgeon imposed similar restrictions across large swathes of Scotland.

Now do I hear "he's an idiot" "he's lost the plot" " can't stand the man" comments? No silence is deafening.

It would appear they only want to nit pick at one of the most respected Politicians in the world and an honest caring , compassionate Scotswoman but ignore the the failings of a proven liar and cheating Tory. Why guys? Luv n Peace and Stay Safe. ⊙✕✕✕✕✕✕✕✕✕✕✕✕✕✕✕✕

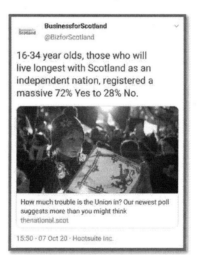

Janey Godley - Frank get the door

https://www.youtube.com/watch?v=qNdMuuF4uDM&list=UURvLN6EjLXIqteezXkpkU4A&index=24

Empire State Building lights up blue for John Lennon's 80th birthday

They turned out in their
Millions to Vote for bojo's
Brexit Circus
now they are finding out,
they are the biggest
Clowns of all

11/10/20. Margaret Ferrier: Covid MP says virus 'makes you act out of character'

FFS....have some dignity and step down.

If what she did wasn't bad enough she now says was actually following Cummings the UK's top adviser's advice.... and was actually driving the train to test her eyesight....

https://www.bbc.co.uk/news/uk-scotland-54496759

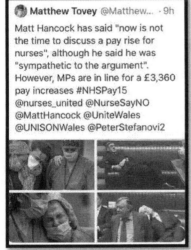 

Corrupt thieving cunts

12/10/20

You not having anything?

David__Osland
@David__Osland

Paying for sex with free school meal vouchers doesn't happen. Paying for sex by giving your girlfriend's tech start-up £120,000 in public money certainly does.

Meanwhile in the House of Commons

Members' Dining Room

Starters

Soup of the day
£2.71

Rosemary salt baked squash panna cotta with almond feta, beer and onion ketchup
and parsnip crisps (Ve) (GF)
£4.10

Balsamic and thyme honey beetroot tartar with golden cross goats' cheese mousse,
Granny Smith apple and micro celery (V) (GF)
£4.10

Pressed duck leg and caper terrine with celeriac and mustard rémoulade
and sour dough toast*
£4.52

Pan seared mackerel with heritage tomato ceviche, elderflower gel, horseradish
and charred cucumber (GF)
£4.52

Traditional prawn cocktail with gem lettuce
and brown bread and butter
£3.25

Mains

Chargrilled ribeye steak with hand cut chips, tomato, mushroom
and Béarnaise sauce (GF)
£9.19

Pan fried salmon with courgette provençale, buttered cocotte potatoes, black olive crumb
and chive cream sauce (GF)
£7.33

Traditional beer battered cod with hand cut chips, mushy peas and tartar sauce
£7.33

Mini sirloin of beef with mini steak and kidney pudding, roasted baby carrots,
savoy cabbage and potato terrine*
£9.19

Slow cooked pork belly with pancetta and root vegetable spelt, crisp kale and salt baked swede*
£8.45

Leek and wild mushroom bread and butter pudding with chargrilled spring onions,
roast celeriac puree and rosemary poached turnip (V)
£7.33

Roasted cauliflower and tarragon steaklet with samphire and hazelnut pesto, pickled kohlrabi
and aubergine baba ganoush (Ve) (GF)
£7.33

Peter Stefanovic ✔
@PeterStefanovi2

"Fighting child hunger is at the core of what we said in our manifesto" says Brandon Lewis days after voting down a motion to prevent a million kids going hungry this Christmas

If it takes my dying breath I shall see these Victorian truth twisting charlatans thrown from office

---

Peter Stefanovic ✔
@PeterStefanovi2

Billions spaffed on failing out sourced test & trace, billions more squandered on no-deal Brexit preparation but no money for hungry kids. This Gov't is as cruel, vile & despicable as it is Victorian

Boris Johnson rejects Marcus Rashford's campaign to extend free school meals
independent.co.uk

Meanwhile in Scotland: Scottish Government provides extra £10m for free school meals

12/10/20. Meanwhile in Scotland :- Nicola Sturgeon said that she would not claim the full salary available to her, She did this as part of a voluntary pay freeze pegging her salary to 2008/9 levels.

A spokesman for Salmond said: "Mr Salmond donated his gross Holyrood salary to a charitable trust to support youth and community causes in the North East of Scotland".

Are You Yes Yet?

13/10/20. Further job losses announced in Edinburgh due to Covid and lockdown......thousands of Romanian street beggars are set to lose their jobs. One called Ivana Geezapounski who didn't want to be named said the "trade has collapsed ...even though my Boss Tomski Kinski got me contactless machine......how am I supposed to feed his 5 kids, a dug and get a new iPhone on UC"? (Lucky I speak Romanian)

Janey Godley – Underskirts and tight shoes.

I agree....let's hope every Tory gets The Clap.

15/10/12. Tens of £Billions have now been handed out to Track and Trace and PPE manufacturers without tender or Due Diligence... that have failed to deliver .....putting thousands of lives at risk. What's the common denominator? They are are handed out by the most corrupt Government the UK has ever witnessed to companies with direct links to Cummings, Whitey, Hancock and Tory Party donors. 😡😡😡😡

Tens of £Billions to line the pockets of already millionaires putting lives at risk but keyboard warriors waste their time nit picking at Sturgeon because she tries to save lives by shutting pubs for 16 days. Take a look in the mirror guys.....where are your morals? Where are your criticisms of Johnson and Co even when he will announce exactly the same measures today? So Sturgeon is "an idiot" but Johnson is your idol? 😂✂✂✂✂✂✂✂✂✂✂✂

Janey Godley - Mute yourself

https://www.youtube.com/watch?v=x8PvOfuWZHo&list=UURvLN6EjLXIqteezXkpkU4A&index =16

 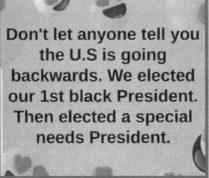

"I went through it and now they say I'm immune," Trump told a cheering crowd in Sanford, near Orlando, few of whom wore masks.

Along with every other corrupt Tory .....I hope. ...❤️✂️✂️✂️✂️✂️✂️✂️✂️

17/10/20. Of course Nicola would never say this.......but I bet she thinks it every minute...❤️✂️✂️✂️✂️✂️✂️✂️

18/10/20. Covid in Europe: second wave gathers pace across continent
France has said it may be forced to impose new lockdowns, **Italy** is expected to ban private parties, and the Czech Republic announced that it would close bars and shift most schools to distance learning as Europe's second wave of Covid-19 continues to gather pace.

Follow OUR Leader. St Nicola ahead of the game as usual 😃😃😃😃😃😃😃

All we have heard from Johnson since March is "we are following the science". Now we find he has ignored his own SAGE who advised 3 week ago unless there was a 2 week total lockdown the result would be "catastrophic consequences"......how the fuck do you ignore "catastrophic consequences?" 😡😡😡😡😡😡

19/10/20. OK deep breaths before I put myself in the firing line but here goes.......

John Leslie dragged into the courts again. This time for allegedly grabbing a woman's breasts at a party in front of witnesses I assume? Totally unacceptable ...if true.

The UNIDENTIFIED woman said in court "I was a bit stunned. I didn't say anything, I was a bit annoyed". Did the UNIDENTIFIED woman remain a bit annoyed for 12 years since it allegedly happened?

I am neither defending John Leslie or condoning any form of sexual assault on a male or female but is this a fair judicial system? If the case is dropped or he is found innocent will the woman be named? No.

I can appreciate the situation can be different in a case of serious assault when identifying the accuser could bring intolerable distress. This woman may have remained "annoyed" for 12 years but if she wants to take the accused to court now should she not be identified? If Leslie is found not guilty only him and his family have suffered from the publicity. If he is found guilty she can sue for damages.

I'm not trying to light the blue touch paper and stand back but would be interested in any female and male friends making comments? Luv n Peace and Stay Safe. 😈

20/10/20.Nicola Sturgeon brands Boris Johnson 'beyond belief' over no-deal

Brexit

The First Minister warned that such a scenario would be "disastrous" for Scotland's beleaguered economy, which is still struggling to recover from the impact of coronavirus.

What happened to Johnsons "Oven Ready Deal?" It wasn't even a microwave ready meal.....more like a 7 day old Toad in His Hole meal.😡😡😡😡😡✗✗✗✗✗✗✗✗

21/10/20. Boris Johnson gets his coronavirus rules wrong again during press conference

The Prime Minister suggested parents and children who live apart may face restrictions if one of their areas goes into heightened controls.

But the moron expects the general public to follow them. 😡😡😡😡😡✗✗✗✗✗✗✗✗

MARK SPENCER
TORY MP FOR SHERWOOD

MARK VOTED TO CUT ESA FOR HIS
SICK & DISABLED CONSTITUENTS

In early 2015 Mark suggested a man
with serious learning difficulties, who
had been left with no food or power for
days on end after being sanctioned for
arriving just 4 MINUTES late at the
benefit office should "learn the
discipline of timekeeping".

Police are currently investigating
Mark's 2015 election expenses
after getting a request for a
12 month extension granted
by the courts.

MARK'S COSTS AND EXPENSE CLAIMS FOR
LAST YEAR WERE £130,855.67 PLUS SALARY

David Schneider ✓
@davidschneider

The government had one job: Prevent a 2nd wave.

They had six months.

They spent £12bn.

They appointed a pal with no expertise as head.

They used private companies not local health authorities.

They fucked it.

Now we're back to where we were in March.

Just so that we don't forget that these Tory cunts were complete inhumane lying cheating bastards long before coronavirus. 🤬🤬🤬🤬🤬✖✖✖✖✖✖✖✖✖

WESTMINSTER IS THE PROBLEM

INDEPENDENCE IS THE SOLUTION

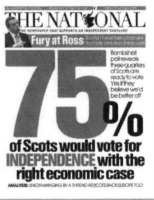

THE NATIONAL
THE NEWSPAPER THAT SUPPORTS AN INDEPENDENT SCOTLAND
Fury at Ross

Bombshell poll reveals three-quarters of Scots are ready to vote Yes if they believe we'd be better off

75%
of Scots would vote for
INDEPENDENCE with the
right economic case

ANALYSIS: UNION HANGING BY A THREAD AS SCOTS BACK EUROPE TOO

22/10/20. Dominic Cummings' £30k unpaid council tax bill 'written off'

Above every law that applies to everyone else. Giving Boris it up the arse obviously pays dividends.

26/10/20 SEVEN week-old firm with links to Tory peer lands £122 million PPE contract

Unsurprisingly, there was no tender process when the contract was handed to an associate of Baroness Mone. Corrupt cunts does not adequately describe depravity of The UK Tory Government

https://www.thelondoneconomic.com/politics/seven-week-old-firm-with-links-to-tory-peer-lands-122-million-ppe-contract/08/10/

04/11/12. Even the House of Lords are calling out Boris Johnson and the Tories on their power grab.

What should we expect? Johnson said in April "we will have a world beating test and trace app" Like most people I thought we would turn to the experts....but no £billions handed over to New Co Private Testicles and Trace.......not because of their expertise....but because Cummings, Whitey and other Boris Bum chums had shares in them. I hate to say it but do you think an Apple/Google/FB collaboration would have saved lives? They kinda know what they are doing when it comes to tracking our every fucking thought and movements....... Yeah of course they would have made huge profits but this is down to saving fucking lives and I kinda think they know what they are doing.....I doubt if their app would say "If you are worried about losing your eyesight immediately put the wife and kids in the car and go for a test drive"
🌑🌑🌑🌑🌑🌑🌑✕✕✕✕✕✕✕✕✕✕

Corrupt cunts does not adequately describe depravity of The UK Tory Government 🌑🌑🌑🌑🌑

Tens of £Billions have now been handed out to Track and Trace and PPE manufacturers without tender or Due Diligence...that have failed to deliver....putting thousands of lives at risk. What is the common denominator? They are handed out by the most corrupt Government the UK has ever witnessed to companies with direct links to Cummings, Hancock, Raab, etc and Tory Party donors among others. 🌑🌑🌑🌑🌑🌑🌑

Are You Yes Yet for an Independent Scotland ? If not don't waste your time posting on here as your opinion is of no relevance to me. 💙✕✕✕✕✕✕✕✕✕✕✕✕✕✕✕✕✕✕✕✕✕✕✕✕

05/11/12. Trump sings Bohemian Rhapsody – pure genius.

https://www.facebook.com/kevin.buxton.754/videos/10157793220547561

05/11/20. Dido Harding: PM and Hancock being sued for handing her Test and Trace role.

https://www.thelondoneconomic.com/politics/dido-harding-pm-and-hancock-being-sued-for-handing-her-test-and-trace-role/02/11/?fbclid=IwAR1TkHY_y7W95Uwj4AkMkI-y5jJqaFozMyKr52MC2hRnUfSxJRzIVO8iWiE

06/11/20. As we're seeing across the Atlantic just now, politicians who rage against democracy don't prevail. Let's not dignify this rubbish. Instead let's keep making and winning the case for independence. Power doesn't belong to politicians - it belongs to the people.

06/11/20. Live from the Whitehouse......

Preview of what could happen in November if.....

https://www.facebook.com/norma.sinclair.75/videos/3352870264766302

Janey Godley - Glasgow Melania

https://www.youtube.com/watch?v=x8PvOfuWZHo&list=UURvLN6EjLXIqteezXkpkU4A&index=16

07/11/20. Hancock labeled "corrupt" after handing another Covid contract to failing private healthcare company.

Is there no end to this Tory corruption that is the cause of thousands of unnecessary deaths due to £millions being handed over to shell companies instead of being given to NHS proven and approved suppliers?

https://www.thelondoneconomic.com/news/hancock-labelled-corrupt-after-handing-another-covid-contract-to-failing-private-healthcare-company/05/11/?fbclid=IwAR1TFNaZ2MCLSQQte3MWX0CHUXZRT4j58pTNcaCwy6ya892VAjf0Nzi7C6I

www.wefail.art

07/11/20. We could speed up no 2's departure......with a sniper......

07/11/20. If you think my posts are annoying, stupid and not funny......bad news....I've got 7 mates! If you have a family member or a friend you dislike why not buy them a copy......and annoy the fuck out them....why should you be the only ones to suffer? 😎 250 pages of jokes, memes, videos, personal insults and full colour flipbook included. 😀😀😀

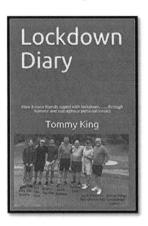

https://www.amazon.co.uk/gp/product/B08L9PF57P/ref=ppx_yo_dt_b_asin_title_o00_s00?ie=UTF8&psc=1&fbclid=IwA R2b2DM-7B42f1gBuVUA7acnanZYByO7zaws9ptlcH5OpnYTTW4fL1TNCW4

Woman sees a sign in a pet shop window......."FANNY LICKING FROG £25"

In she goes "I'd like to see the fanny licking frog please?" Bloke behind the counter hopes over and says "Bonjour".

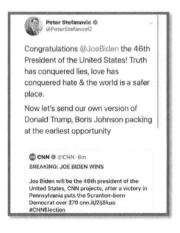

08/11/20. Mum doing her bit while Dad toiled down pit. 😊✖️🖼️

9/11/12 .Before his death Sean Connery was described as "Scotland's Greatest Scot". With no disrespect to any actor, singer or any other media personality or even other sportsmen but Ken Buchanan and especially George Kerr have a achieved a level of greatness that is beyond only a few individuals. Proud to know them both. 😢

https://www.youtube.com/watch?v=9IP2VD6vGG4&feature=share&fbclid=IwAR2ST-uDnkUjSG4yjI-aJ_8073HOJsgKglliY6r5iZJAGZObKX30wq-SxMc

Janey Godley - The vaccine

https://www.youtube.com/watch?v=_mdRA2ZE9g0&list=UURvLN6EjLXIqteezXkpkU4A&index=5

11/11/20. Covid: UK first country in Europe to pass 50,000 deaths.

Boris Johnson declares himself 'very proud' of coronavirus response. This was the Moronic Cunt's response to Kier Stammer at PM's QT. 👻

https://www.bbc.co.uk/news/uk-54905018?fbclid=IwAR2vvXl3pGoX2zPg_rNyJBL7-GUITHkqHQZzmttxG-vN2nCbqwa-OJRqumw

12/11/20. ROBERT JENRICK - Government Suppress Key Documents from MPs in *Constituency Payoff Scandal*

I now think the establishment is overloading us with Tory corruption in the hope that we will all just accept it as the norm and not get angry. Fuck you 😡😡😡😡😡

https://bylinetimes.com/2020/11/11/robert-jenrick-boris-johnsons-government-suppress-key-documents-from-mps-in-constituency-kick-back-scandal/?fbclid=IwAR3Ps-tS90RGhVqtM7Pwwz113nz4Ps7F4RZnZrNryr7IE5p2aYetZ1UISTO

13/11/20. Dominic Cummings quits Downing Street.

Well that's a fuckin shame but why was he there in the first place? More importantly why was he there after the law breaking Barnard Castle trip breaking the Governments own guidelines and the even more ridiculous "short drive to test my eyesight" statement? Simple really....if you are a corrupt, lying cunt you can rely on another corrupt, lying, cheating cunt that gave the job in the first place to back you up. 😡😡😡😡😡❌

https://www.lbc.co.uk/politics/dominic-cummings-quits-downing-street/?fbclid=IwAR0pNZ1Mu6mjAC_bKEY0kAPfy7toytS7czcKdIf2BYhR03gTpHBMSWA3wjA

Janey Godley - Frank get the door

https://www.youtube.com/watch?v=1NnQa8UhlzQ&list=UURvLN6EjLXIqteezXkpkU4A&index=

3

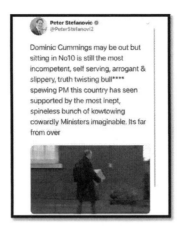

12/11/20. I feel I need to correct Peter Stefanovic in calling Johnson "the most incompetent, self serving, arrogant & slippery, truth twisting bull**** spewing PM this country has seen".......he missed out lying. cheating cunt. ⬤✕✕✕✕✕✕✕✕✕✕

12/11/20. A Glasgow girl writes to the problem page in The Sun......"Dear Frank, I am a 14 year old Celtic Fan and I'm still a virgin............Do you think my brothers are gay?"

13/11/20. My friend's wife left him last week. She said she was going to the shops for milk and never came back.

I asked him how he was coping. He said "Not bad. I've been using some of that powdered stuff". 🐄

13/11/20. SNP claims Dominic Cummings has done 'irreparable damage' to Tories and UK

.......although I don't think Dumbcunt Cummings has really done any more damage than Thatcher, Johnson and every other Tory PM and supporter has done to humanity. ⬤✕✕✕✕✕✕✕✕✕✕✕✕✕✕✕✕

https://www.scotsman.com/news/politics/snp-claims-dominic-cummings-has-done-irreparable-damage-tories-and-uk-3034972?fbclid=IwAR0PNt81E0BEH5dU7wv73jd9_HvYW3XaQCBiyGrRPMnf6B5DzglDxxqJOII

14/11/20. I feel I need to correct Peter Stefanovic in calling Johnson the most incompetent, self serving, arrogant & slippery, truth twisting bull**** spewing PM this country has seen.......he missed out lying, cheating cunt. 😷✂️✂️✂️✂️✂️✂️✂️✂️✂️

14/11/20. RIP Peter Sutcliffe; At his peak probably the best attacker Leeds have produced for a decade.😎

14/11/20. It's jist no fair......

14/11/20 The lies, falsehoods and misrepresentations of Boris Johnson and his government.

It's a bit like "The Boy Who Cried Wolf".

This cunt lies so often his lies are ignored. 😠😠😠😠😠⚔

https://boris-johnson-
lies.com/?fbclid=IwAR2LpLqSdvrAEwYupHU8xCb5ZTmCKnt0UD82Zt03PGjU6LB6p71ILyxOwSE

Janey Godley - My nerves were shattered Nicola Sturgeon on Scotland win.

https://www.youtube.com/watch?v=_mw2CwtPvnM&list=UURvLN6EjLXIqteezXkpkU4A&inde

x=4

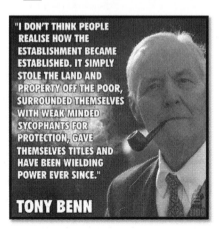

"I DON'T THINK PEOPLE REALISE HOW THE ESTABLISHMENT BECAME ESTABLISHED. IT SIMPLY STOLE THE LAND AND PROPERTY OFF THE POOR, SURROUNDED THEMSELVES WITH WEAK MINDED SYCOPHANTS FOR PROTECTION, GAVE THEMSELVES TITLES AND HAVE BEEN WIELDING POWER EVER SINCE."

TONY BENN

15/11/20.

Wembley tickets

England v Scotland

June 2021

This may be of interest to you. A friend of mine has two tickets in a corporate box for England v Scotland. He paid £300 each, but he didn't realise when he bought them that it was going to be the same day as his Covid 19 postponed wedding. If you are interested, he is looking for someone to take his place.

It's at Kirkcaldy Registry Office, at 2.30pm. The bride's name is Moira, she's 5'4", about 8 stone, quite pretty, has her own income and is a really good cook. ❤✂✂✂✂✂✂✂✂✂✂✂✂

Tom London
@TomLondon6

People don't grasp how much more a billion is than a million

A billion is a THOUSAND million

A million seconds is 11.6 DAYS BUT a billion seconds is 31.7 YEARS

Where has the £12 BILLION handed over for the failed Test and Trace gone?

I strongly suspect more ELITE CORRUPTION

WE NEED TO STOP MEASURING "THE ECONOMY" BY HOW WELL RICH PEOPLE ARE DOING.

16/11/20. It's almost impossible to grasp the catastrophic mess the UK is now in....with The Tory government plunging it deeper and deeper with every minute they are left in charge making catastrophic decisions and then lying to try and cover their mistakes.

The moronic PM who allegedly nearly died from coronavirus is now self isolating because he did not follow his own fucking guidelines.

His pathetic video this morning boasting that he is in self isolation due to the success of NHS Test & Trace means he was in close contact for more than 15 minutes with someone who subsequently tested positive. If you had nearly died from coronavirus and even if you are a complete moron would you not be ultra careful and at least follow your own guidelines that has put the country into lockdown? Clearly not as the pictures show him and the infected MP NOT wearing masks and NOT socially distancing.

Then we have Second in Command Moron, HandCock, THE HEALTH MINISTER being slaughtered on GMB for boycotting a major news channel FOR 6 MTHS during a HEALTH pandemic.

All this while the UK faces a law breaking catastrophic no deal Brexit and the two main architects of Brexit, Cain and not so Able Cummings like rats deserting the sinking UK ship they holed in the first place.

We need emergency legislation to prevent these incompetent moronic Tory cunts killing even more UK citizens. 🤬🤬🤬🤬🤬🤬❌❌❌❌❌❌❌❌❌❌

16/11/12. It's such an easy mistake to make....if you are a corrupt Tory cunt. 🤬🤬🤬🤬🤬❌❌

16/11/12. Breaking News – Due to the uncertainty of Driving Home for Christmas Chris Rea has set off early..........Yeah like the rest of us....not heading home for Christmas............but on "The Road to Hell".....

16/11/20.   He's used his well......

16/11/20. I'm hosting a charity event for people who struggle to reach orgasm. It's next Thursday at 8 pm. If you can't come let me know. If you can make it .....try not to come too early. 😏✂️

16/11/20. Piers Morgan's takedown of Matt Hancock over his Covid-19 record is simply blistering.

I can't stand Morgan but at least he slaughters them the way they deserve. This is Matt HandCock the HEALTH Minister who along with all other Tory MP's has boycotted a major UK news channel for 6 mths during a HEALTH Pandemic. When do you expect the HEALTH Minister to earn his salary and inform the public if it's not during a HEALTH crisis? Disgusting, disgraceful dereliction of duty.😡😡😡😡😡😡😡😡😡😡😡

Follow OUR Leader. 🗡🗡🗡🗡🗡🗡🗡🗡

https://www.thepoke.co.uk/2020/11/16/piers-morgans-takedown-of-matt-hancock-over-covid-19-record-simply-blistering/?fbclid=IwAR1hNnT6QrC7WktWV2RuZ2rOP-XWfgEVale0qVc0ERKDLEQF9PQoFw0yBtg

17/11/20. This moronic, lying, cheating bastard Johnson has caused the unnecessary deaths of hundreds of thousands of UK citizens through "austerity", has led the UK into a Brexit abys and is directly responsible for the UK having the highest number coronavirus deaths of any EU country and one of the highest in the world.

He was allegedly close to death after contacting coronavirus yet goes on to ignore the advice he is enforcing on the public by attending meetings without face masks or social distancing. He is now forced to self isolate and has put himself and other cabinet ministers at risk of being incapacitated or worse at a time the UK is in the midst of the worst crisis in history and should be being led by a strong, honest, caring UK PM. He is exactly the opposite.

The idiotic moron then releases a "trump esque" video bouncing around with a childish grin on his puss claiming he is as fit as butchers dog and full of antibodies. A great comfort to the people that have lost loved ones and their livelihoods due to his actions.

Johnsons views, opinions and actions are disgusting and irrelevant to anyone that is a humanitarian ....regardless of their political views. 😡😡

17/11/20. Boris Johnson triggers Scottish fury and clash with Sturgeon after 'branding devolution a disaster'

This moronic, lying, cheating bastard Johnson has caused the unnecessary deaths of hundreds of thousands of UK citizens through "austerity", has led the UK into a Brexit abyss and is directly responsible for the UK having the highest number coronavirus deaths of any EU country and one of the highest in the world.

He was allegedly close to death after contacting coronavirus yet goes on to ignore the advice he is enforcing on the public by attending meetings without face masks or social distancing. He is now forced to self isolate and has put himself and other cabinet ministers at risk of being incapacitated or worse at a time the UK is in the midst of the worst crisis in history and should be being led by a strong, honest, caring UK PM. He is exactly the opposite.

The idiotic moron then releases a "trump esque" video bouncing around with a childish grin on his puss claiming he is as fit as butchers dog and full of antibodies. A great comfort to the people that have lost loved ones and their livelihoods due to his actions.

Johnson's views, opinions and actions are disgusting and irrelevant to anyone that is a humanitarian ....regardless of their political views.

https://news.sky.com/story/boris-johnson-triggers-scottish-fury-and-clash-with-sturgeon-after-branding-devolution-a-disaster-12134368?fbclid=IwAR0XBYGwWnEFuLAlRYNSIyUuAnLgUWDuBccP8s_rsbouyyFxe3XWcrH60zl

17/11/20. What is the point of Rooth The Mooth, Rennie and Leonard wasting their breath and the FM's time with stupid rhetorical questions........"Can the FM guarantee that these measures will work?"

Of course she can't ya bunch of useless pricks.....but she can try to save lives.

Leonard unfortunately sounds as if he is a sandwich short of a picnic....."Can the FM guarantee that Santa will be able to visit every chimney in Scotland this Christmas regardless of what Tier they are in? Does the FM appreciate that thousands of glasses of milk will go sour and thousands of carrots will rot? Personally, if I don't receive my new X Box I'll be pure ragin and will kick her right in the Fud"

17/11/20. Go-between paid £21m in taxpayer funds for NHS PPE

Only Tory bastards could vote not to provide free school meals for starving children while creating millionaires and possibly billionaires through sheer corruption putting more lives at risk.😡😡😡😡

https://www.bbc.co.uk/news/uk-54974373?fbclid=IwAR2LQq0QVad6Sq2bxck7NHLdf_pPP9QTJox4AF6l3KevcYJIlAgN2ILh5zQ

Janey Godley. "Well that's Glasgow and 10 other councils in tier 4 and Edinburgh is being smug"

https://www.youtube.com/watch?v=Yf8beJoUGGw

18/11/20. Breaking News. Edinburgh Clowncil have raised the threat level in the Meadowbank area from "Nae chance" to "imminent ". To prevent terrorist car bomb attacks they have surrounded two benches where nae cunt has ever been seen sitting with a ring of steel. Big Shug Binladen from Niddry Taliban confirmed the threat. "Aye some cunts getting it.....we're fed up of every bastard wearing masks fur nae reason. We canny tell the honest shoplifters from the shirtlifters. 😊😊

18/11/20. Covid-19: Boris Johnson and six Tory MPs self-isolating after No 10 meeting.

Coronavirus: Head of NHS Test and Trace Dido Harding self-isolating.

Question: How many family or friends do you have that have been contacted requesting them to self isolate? A. I thankfully have none.

However, I know of Boris, another 6 Tory fuds and Dildo Hardon have been.

Conclusion. Dildo and the fuds have not been socially distancing.

So if you have video evidence of Dildo and Fud's coming together please message me. 😊😊

Johnson vs Dildo		
Does the job it's supposed to	✖	✔
Capable of satisfaction	✖	✔
Reliable	✖	✔
Fake	✔	✔
Is a real cock!	✔	✖

OK, so I can't be President any more. No problem, I gonna be Queen. I will be a great Queen, best Queen ever!

It's the only Theory of Einstein I understand......

20/11/20. Not So Priti Person Patel was effectively sacked from her role as UK International Development Secretary and in her own words said her actions "fell below the standards of transparency and openness".
So how the fuck was she appointed Home Secretary?

Oh hang on.... got it.....she was appointed by a corrupt moronic PM who does not have any standards of transparency and openness.

So what will the moronic corrupt PM do now that she is guilty of breaking ministerial standards against staff bullying? Priti obvious really....she will become Minister for Upholding Ministerial Standards.

20/11/20. Not So Pretty Person Patel......if you don't mean to cause offence why is your insincere puss on my telly? 😡

20/12/20. Win a date with Priti Patel

I'd rather stick my cock in the bacon slicer. Actually I got sacked from my first job for doing exactly that......to be fair the butcher did sack the bacon slicer too....

https://www.thedailymash.co.uk/politics/win-a-date-with-priti-patel-20200227193851?fbclid=IwAR2Pe4wBRXlTo4cvN4olNXv9ZFM0PH2P-pLjhFF8yVI1x8I4Ga20xfC1OHk

Boris Johnson #StayAlertCont... ···
@GetBrexit_Done

I tried really hard to sack **Priti Patel** for breaking the ministerial code, but she twisted my arm behind my back, said, "Shut the fuck up, fat boy" and stole my dinner money

22:31 · 19/11/2020 · Twitter Web App

20/11/20. I must admit I felt a little guilty watching the news tonight. Sometimes we forget how lucky we are and ignore the life changing events that other people live through. I must admit I was reduced to tears tonight as I came to terms with the trauma that WAGS endure. Yes Rooney v Vardy............tears were running down my cheeks at the thought of two multi millionaire bints being dragged through the high court because she said but I said she said I said.....a swift boot in the fud to both you....delivered by Rooney and Vardy. 😎

21/11/20. Did you know it's illegal to have anal sex in Iceland?

Not sure about Asda yet.......

Peter Stefanovic ✓
@PeterStefanovi2

Matt Hancock basically telling #BBCBreakfast viewers that if Boris Johnson is happy to have ministers in cabinet that have broken the ministerial code it's ok with him. We've never seen such a bunch of spineless, cowardly cabbage head ministers in Government

07:48 · 11/20/20 · Twitter for iPhone

Peter Stefanovic you have overstepped the line.......how dare you insult cabbages.......

From this..........."This is tough but we can be optimistic that science will get us out of this pandemic"

To this.........

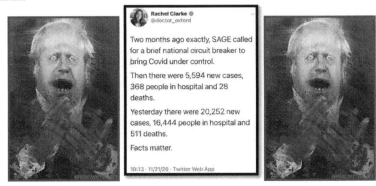

> **Rachel Clarke** ●
> @doctor_oxford
>
> Two months ago exactly, SAGE called for a brief national circuit breaker to bring Covid under control.
>
> Then there were 5,594 new cases, 368 people in hospital and 28 deaths.
>
> Yesterday there were 20,252 new cases, 16,444 people in hospital and 511 deaths.
>
> Facts matter.
>
> 10:13 · 11/21/20 · Twitter Web App

23/11/20. From "operation last gasp"..." hands, face....and total fucking waste of space"...to now "squeeze the disease" .."this is not the season to be jolly.....but season to be jolly careful"...should the moronic cunt not put more thought into saving lives than smart arsed advertising slogans? Does he think that making two words rhyme impresses us? 😡😡

23/11/20. Oxford AstraZeneca Covid vaccine has up to 90% efficiency.

Great news for everyone but who should be prioritised for the first 4 million doses?

One of of reasons the UK has the highest coronavirus death rates in the world was the UK Government's initial disastrous response of Herd Immunity route which can only be effective if there is a vaccine. Now we appear to have vaccines the Government is indicating the initial 4 million vaccine doses will be given to the elderly. Now Ah dinnie want to push yer Granny off the bus before it's her stop.....but should the priority not be NHS front line staff risking their lives every day? Just asking. 💬🔪

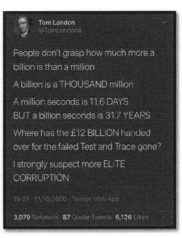

Cost of track and trace system:

Ireland £773,000

United Kingdom £12,000,000,000

Guess which one works?

#wato #bbcwato #ToryCorruption

Tom London
@TomLondon8

People don't grasp how much more a billion is than a million

A billion is a THOUSAND million

A million seconds is 11.6 DAYS
BUT a billion seconds is 31.7 YEARS

Where has the £12 BILLION handed over for the failed Test and Trace gone?

I strongly suspect more ELITE CORRUPTION

19:27 · 17/10/2020 · Twitter Web App

3,079 Retweets 87 Quote Tweets 6,126 Likes

24/11/20. How many Tory £millionaires have been created from the £12,000,000,000? More importantly how many lives could have been saved if that £12,000,000,000 had been properly pumped into NHS front line for proper PPE from legitimate manufacturers along with ventilators instead of Dyson's?

United Kingdom Deaths: 61,245 – The highest death toll in Europe.

China Deaths: 4,634 ???? – Diane Abbot was in charge of the count.

26/12/20. Matt Hancock ripped to shreds over MP's Pay Rise.

The bastard just smirks and refuses to answer why MP's deserve a pay rise and Front line workers don't.

https://www.facebook.com/watch/?v=192117245818847

27/11/20. First Minister's Questions.....we are in the midst of a world crisis......could Rooth the Mooth...just shut the fuck up about a relatively meaningless enquiry. Nobody will die if this is put on the back burner. 💀

27/11/20. I believe there will be a large majority for YES especially if Indy 2 is during 2021. Nicola Sturgeons honest, caring and passionate handling of the Covid crisis compared to the UK governments bumbling incompetent, corrupt and fatally catastrophic actions will have swayed many towards Independence.

My biggest fear is electoral fraud. The very obvious level of corruption this government is capable off is a clear indication that there is nothing they will not stoop to for their own perceived gain.

There is irrefutable evidence of electoral fraud at Indy 1, Brexit and the Dec 2019 UK election.

I doubt if Johnson can survive after his handling of the Covid crisis is truly examined. A YES vote will be the final nail in his coffin.....literally.

Under the bridge at Glasgow Central tonight. Queue for soup kitchen. Welcome to Tory Brexit Britain, where the streets are paved with shite.

28/11/20. I'm sure Johnson and the multiple £millionaires & £billionaires he has created by handing his corrupt buddy's cash for non existent PPE will be devastated to see life in the real world they have created........will they FUCK....they will be laughing all the way to their offshore tax havens with their blood money. CUNTS.

30/11/20. As an experiment my wife has been wearing an "I LOVE Boris badge" and a blue Tory rosette. So far she has been spat on, kicked, punched and headbutted.....fuck knows what will happen if she leaves the house.

30/11/20. Breaking News...Boris .Johnson slams Nicola Sturgeon's plans to gift Scottish families £100 at Christmas. He said "This is a clear attempt by Scotland's FM to undermine credibility in the UK Government and make the Government look like morally corrupt selfish cunts......that is my job not hers"

30/11/20. Edinburgh Castle lights up blue to celebrate Scotland's Patron Saint

A wonderful sight right in the heart of our city. The Castle is lit up blue this evening to celebrate St Andrew's Day. ▨▨▨▨▨▨▨▨▨▨

01/12/20/ Philip Green's Arcadia on brink of collapse, putting 13,000 jobs at risk

Unfortunately the bastard will still be a £Billionaire after fucking up the lives of thousands of ordinary workers by theft and corruption....the reason he is a Tory "Sir". 🙂🙂🙂🙂🙂🙂🙂🙂🙂🙂

https://www.theguardian.com/business/2020/nov/27/philip-green-arcadia-on-brink-of-collapse-putting-15000-jobs-at-risk-covid

01/12/20. Scotch egg is definitely a substantial meal, says Michael Gove.

Following the outcry over free school meals....UK Government announces it will be providing "one substantial meal" per family completely free ......to any household with six or more children....."

After I've had my Scotch egg I'm going to wrap some xmas prezzies using Scotch tape, then go and buy The Scotsman to read on The Flying Scotsman on my way up north to shoot wild haggis in the Scottish Highlands. What do we have to associate with the south east of Englandshire? Oh yeah...Toads in their Holes and Morris Prancing....

https://www.theguardian.com/world/2020/dec/01/scotch-egg-is-definitely-a-substantial-meal-says-michael-gove?CMP=fb_gu&utm_medium=Social&utm_source=Facebook&fbclid=IwAR27TDCQYmj2YhInc6ix9I0BU1TygE4Pkar1Cuh7Ve_mqKsZy1ffrKnRtJk#Echobox=1606823457

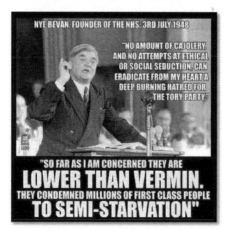

01/12/20. Vote for a fairer caring society.

01/12/20. The neighbor and former landlord of Matt Hancock's local pub won government orders worth at least £30 million for supplying vials for coronavirus tests.

Breaking news.....publican puts his Cock Inn Hand Cock. FFS how many £millionaires have these Tory cunts created in this crisis? 😡😡😡

https://www.thetimes.co.uk/edition/news/matt-hancocks-neighbour-won-30m-deal-to-supply-vials-for-covid-tests-gnsbg8vgx?utm_medium=Social&utm_source=Facebook&fbclid=IwAR32jNpCIkoJGLx8ndXS4CqAR_JYQ0-Wi9GiuMEibczIYIWiHx4bk1t3uJU#Echobox=1606461687

01/12/20. If you enjoy horror movies based on true stories then I recommend "The Social Dilemma" on Netflix. Watch it and I guarantee 3 things if you have a brain and can think for yourself.

1) It will scare you shitless.
2) You will decide to delete FB and all other social media apps.
3) You will not do 2).

Why? Because we are addicts. Unlike alcohol, weed, heroin, coke and all other addictions we would not want to admit to, all our close family and close friends are also addicts so there is no shame. What you will realise that this addiction is influencing your every thought, action, purchase, vote and literally the world we live in. Luv n Peace and stay safe. 😎😎😎😎

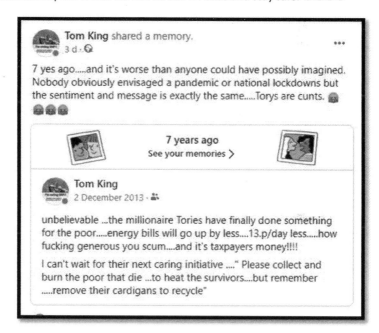

02/12/20.

02/12/20. Expect a smug puss PM stressing the UK is the first country in the World to roll out a vaccine. Will he mention that it's not yet approved in Belgium where it's manufactured? 🤔

Is Monica Lewinsky trying a new PR stunt?

04/12/20. Gavin Williamson tells LBC the UK approved a Covid vaccine first because 'we're a much better country' than France, Belgium and the US.

Oh yeah? Created by German scientists and manufactured in Belgium Ya Smug Arsehole.

https://twitter.com/LBC/status/1334463894388170753

05/12/20. Jonathan Van-Tam launches train analogy at Covid briefing

Where the fuck do they get these arseholes? Does he think he is talking to a naughty child refusing to eat his greens? "open up the tunnel here comes the broccoli choo choo..."

And why the fuck would you use a train analogy in the UK about delivering a life saving vaccine? "Unfortunately the 14:00 hr life saving covid train is delayed due to the wrong type of snow.....it's now expected 20:30.....the year not the hour.

https://www.dailymail.co.uk/news/article-9011083/Social-media-goes-overdrive-Jonathan-Van-Tam-launches-train-analogy.html

Janey Godley - The fridges

https://www.youtube.com/watch?v=OzGpM14iu5Q

At least he's got some equipment ....obviously Failing Grayling didn't have a say in this one......

The vaccine must be stored and transported at low temperature by specialist firms...

YIPPEE! its Mr.Whippy

Luckily a neighbour of the Health Minister has the relevant equipment & has been awarded a £20 billion contract.

Rosie Moore
@RosieMoore1993

All politics aside, this woman has led us through what can only be described as an absolute shit-show of a year. A woman who has a family and a life too. I cannot even fathom what it requires to lead this country at the moment, but my God I'm grateful. Thankyou. @NicolaSturgeon

08/12/20. Can't believe Sturgeon has got is so wrong and kept Edinburgh in Tier 3.

I mean who the fuck does she think is...the elected FM of Scotland or something? Eh.

It must be so easy making decisions about who might live and who might die eh? I mean that Johnson seems to be spot on and gets it right every time eh? There's even loads on here that think they could dae better eh?

Ah bet the selfish bitch disnie even go tae the pub eh? And that's all that's important eh?

Ah think you should all protest - tell they nurses tae hand back their £500 Christmas bonus, tell the bairns their no huvin any her fuckin free meals, tell her wie dinnie want her fuckin free prescriptions and best of all tell her ti stick hur free fanny pads up hur erse.

We want Boris eh? We should all be revolting......although some on here already are.... 😎

09/12/20. This Year's Oscar for worst ever "trying to fake" emotion goes to....Matt HandCock.... How the fuck does any human cry and smirk at the same time? Simplze....the cunt's a Tory not a human. 💩

https://www.facebook.com/TheIndependentOnline/videos/185428513292366/?__cft__[0]=AZX4HfYYPy4p0wkPcNr2C3 uAnSEoMN2MWik1zpsDm4atx_ISGecIZPLGq18gNNvl8AWGiYQAxNhe2vWnelU1poZzrNQa38-V2UuC8- pek8X9DmASctuu4v_odnl9KGVZOQo&__tn__=-UK-R

Spirit of Scotland

In the year 2021

Scotland's Independence will be won

There will be freedom from Tory rule for everyone

Say YES for a Fairer Caring Scotland

By Tommy King

A young Scouse woman was so depressed that she decided to launch herself into the Mersey, but just before she did a handsome young man stopped her.

"You have so much to live for," said the man. "I'm a sailor and we are off to Australia tomorrow. I can stow you away on my ship. I'll take care of you, bring you food every day and keep you happy."

With nothing to lose and the prospect of going to Australia, the woman accepted. That night the sailor brought her aboard and hid her in a small but comfortable compartment in the hold. From then on every night he would bring her three sandwiches, a bottle of red wine and make love to her until dawn.

Two weeks later she was discovered by the captain during a routine inspection. "What are you doing here?" asked the captain.

"I have an arrangement with one of the sailors," she replied. "He brings me food and I get a free trip to Australia."

"I see," the captain says.

Her conscience got the best of her and she added, "Plus, he's screwing me."

"He certainly is," replied the captain. "This is the Birkenhead ferry." — 😎😊😊😊😊

09/12/20. Unionist NAWBAG thinking on Sturgeon...."She is just using her broadcasts and decisions to win votes and become popular" ....she gets slaughtered by them for leaving Edinburgh in Tier 3....."She is just using her broadcasts and decisions to lose votes and become unpopular"...??? ...a recent study showed that 20% of Unionists were on medication for schizophrenia which is very worrying.....80% of the cunts are not on proper medication.....😎

09/12/20. Very news sad that many England players can't remember winning the 1966 World Cup or the Rugby World Cup in 2003.......that's only 50,000,000 of their supporters to go....😎

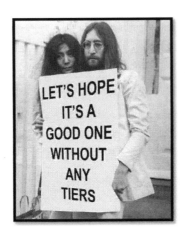

11/12/20. Watching Baroness Colonel Ruth von Mooth seething today, noting her deeply puckered mouth, reminded me of an expression my dear old Mum was wont to use. "Look at that pucker faced cow," she'd say, "She's got a mooth like an erse."

11/12/20. I should be used to it by now...SKY News priorities...."Throughout today we will be looking back over the career of a British icon and star of the Carry on farces....PLUS we will look at the possible effects of a NO Deal Brexit on the UK economy....". Should it not have opened with.."Throughout today we will be looking back over the career of a British Arsehole and star of the Carry on UK farces and the catastrophic effects of a No deal Brexit........"

I suppose it was also asking too much to mention "The Kay Burley show will be presented by various stand- in presenters for the next six months.....who will continue Kay Burley's infamous way of embarrassing MP's over breaking coronavirus guidelines.....due to her breaking coronavirus guidelines....."

11/12/20. LIES, LIES and DAMNED LIES : THE BORIS JOHNSON COLLECTION.

Boris Johnson: insults, gaffes and apologies.

https://www.youtube.com/watch?v=bLk5aEZKHcA

Boris Johnson denies lying to the Queen.

https://www.youtube.com/watch?v=6QwV1_MuXZA

Boris Johnson's record of lying makes him unfit to be PM, says Chuka Umunna

https://www.youtube.com/watch?v=Xk61GRgGaGU

Boris Johnson caught out over lies about Turkey.

https://www.youtube.com/watch?v=Yq_DApu4HiI

Boris Johnson Lies to get out of being caught out lying.

https://www.youtube.com/watch?v=gmZO0tucdbY

Boris Johnson to face court over Brexit lies.

https://www.youtube.com/watch?v=XWs8GxCu3IE

Boris Johnson has made a career out of lying, says SNP's Ian Blackford.

https://www.youtube.com/watch?v=OiuUmvDebes

Go straight to Hell

11/12/2-. More shocking evidence has emerged that Boris Johnson deliberately conflated the withdrawal agreement with a trade deal to deceive voters

https://www.facebook.com/watch/?v=375309460436362&notif_id=1607795397872512&notif_t=watch_follower_video&ref=notif

11/12/20. This was disgraceful from BBC Politics live! It's not your job to say what the Prime Minister is thinking when promoting his "oven ready deal." It's not your job to tell viewers he was talking about the withdrawal agreement & not a trade deal! Show viewers this & let them decide!

https://www.facebook.com/156333781415919/videos/2971792063079212

11/12/20. Scottish independence in the spotlight during Nicola Sturgeon's CNN interview

https://www.thenational.scot/news/18936955.scottish-independence-spotlight-nicola-sturgeons-cnn-interview/?fbclid=IwAR0JHcfWgcXdo3AOWtCCLLu3oS066S2cUNM2UsO8vP_JnvTmQ2awQhuLt38

13/12/20. UK warns it may not buy electricity from an independent Scotland

Another blatant scare tactic from the unionist establishment in the run up to Indy 2.

Scotland is on target to deliver the equivalent of **100%** of gross electricity consumption from renewable. 2020 was a record for renewable electricity generation in Scotland with a new record high in Q1 2020, with 11.6 TWh generated between January and March 2020. A Scotland split from Britain would have to rely on electricity exports to the United Kingdom to sell excess renewable energy generation because its grid is connected only with England and, to a lesser extent, Northern Ireland. Britain also imports electricity from the Netherlands, France and Ireland and plans to build other links to Belgium, Norway and Denmark. However, as Scotland will become self sufficient it will be better placed to export cheaper electricity to the rest of the UK than other countries especially EU countries when England is out of the EU. Unfortunately, as there will still be a Tory Government at the time of Indy 2, Scotland needs to prepare for the war the UK media will launch with lies, fake news and illegal social media tactics. Let's make sure the YES vote is so overwhelming it will be impossible for them to win the war and Scotland will be free from Tory rule for ever and become a prosperous fairer caring society.

21/12/20. The Trials and Triumphs of Nicola Sturgeon.

If 2020 was a tale of two cities, for Nicola Sturgeon in Edinburgh it really was the best of times and the worst of times. Like Boris Johnson in London, she began the year fresh from electoral triumph with a thumping majority. Then Covid struck, bringing unimaginable horror. The virus shattered Johnson's popularity, but elevated Sturgeon's approval ratings to a level that could rewrite the future of the United Kingdom. The first minister of Scotland may well look back on this as the year her lifelong dream of independence finally began to come true.

https://www.thetimes.co.uk/article/the-trials-and-triumphs-of-nicola-sturgeon-52htwbs2b

It's now imperative that PM seeks an agreement to extend the Brexit transition period. The new Covid strain - & the various implications of it - means we face a profoundly serious situation, & it demands our 100% attention. It would be unconscionable to compound it with Brexit.

https://www.facebook.com/andrew.buchan.505/videos/3859746144057123

22/12/20. Not Pritti Person Patel obviously went to the same acting classes a Hancock,

Lesson 1). Smirk and look smug as fuck while repeating what a great job the Government has done while refusing to answer the question.
Lesson 2). Smirk and look smug as fuck while repeating what a great job the Government has done while refusing to answer the question.
Lesson 3). Smirk and look smug as fuck while repeating what a great job the Government has done while refusing to answer the question.
Lesson 4). Smirk and look smug as fuck while repeating what a great job the Government has done while refusing to answer the question.

Next week she will attend the "How not to cry while crying at the same time as Smirking and look smug as fuck while repeating what a great job the Government has done while refusing to answer the question".

22/12/20. If you are confused about the rate corona virus can spread and what the "R" number means think of this - if you place 1 grain of sand on the first square of a chess board then 2 on the second then 4 on the third and keep doubling how many grains are on the 64th square? Answer - 9,223,372,036,854,775,808.

So basically, if Wee Shug is infected and goes to meet Big Agnes in the pub and infects her and then they go and meet 2 pals in the next pub and go and meet 4 pals in the next pub but go on a 64 pub, pub crawl.... there would be 9,223,372,036,854,775,808 drunk cunts looking for a fight i.e... the world is fucked. STAY HOME 🖤

23/12/20. I don't agree the hospitality industry has been unfairly treated in the crisis. Although the vast majority of pubs etc have been very strict in adhering to guidelines the nature of the beast is still alcohol. People in pubs are more relaxed, talk closer face to face, shout and sing more than they tend to do walking down the aisle in Tesco. We know what happened in Aberdeen but closer to home the Iona Bar was caught serving alcohol to around 70 Hibs casuals in the street requiring a huge police presence to shut them down. I was in one of my own west end locals on the same day two people tested positive but neither the bar or NHS contacted me.... I read about it on FB. Complete lockdown for as long as it takes is the only way to defeat this nightmare. Of course, it's tough but I speak as someone who lives alone, who's business/income in hospitality and social life have been decimated. I am still way more grateful for my situation than millions with children at home, big mortgages, loans etc especially if they are in the hospitality industry but if we are going to be around to celebrate next Christmas with family and friends then we are going to suffer now but that suffering will be much greater if we don't take action. Luv n Peace and Stay Safe. 😊

23/12/20. 774 UK Covid deaths yesterday.....I remember thinking back in March that people were scaremongering and being ridiculous talking about 1,000 deaths per day.....Johnson was warned in September by his own advisers that full lockdown was required to prevent a "catastrophic" death rate of plus 4,000 per day.

As we now head for full lockdown Matt Hancock says "the key to defeating this virus to act quickly".....in case he is leaving the counting to Diane Abbott......that warning was 90 days ago.

23/12/20. Janey Godley - "Totally f* it" Nicola took off her mask at a wake**

https://www.facebook.com/janeygodleyfanpage/videos/1102017410254376

As usual Janey gets her message across with humour. Yes, Nicola Sturgeon had a momentary lapse in judgement removing her mask but the MSM headlines would have you belive it was a deliberate attempt to infect and kill the three old wives.......forgetting that is exactly the plan that Cummings and Johnson implemented in March.

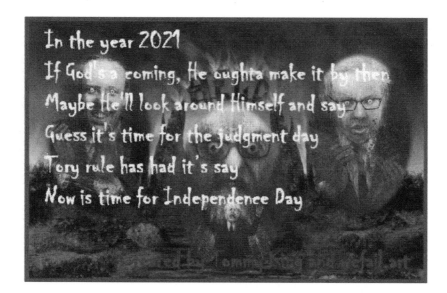

Now is time for Independence Day

In the Year 2021 Scotland's Independence will be Won There will be Freedom from Tory rule for everyone................ Say YES for a Fairer Caring Society
by Tommy King

24/12/20. My friend Grants fun "Save lives" ditty.

https://www.facebook.com/grant.stott.94/videos/10160665466964535

25/12/20.

To All my Family and Friends I hope 2021 is a great one And is just Tickity Boo for You Love Tommy

www.tickityboo.club

Coming soon

25/12/20. The KKK....King Kute Klan. 🖤🖤

Christmas is normally a time of year to spend time with family and friends but not this year. I would normally have one day with my son and daughter at their mums and another day with my sister and the rest of her family. I was concerned when the initial 5 day lifting of restrictions was announced that it was too long and discussed with everyone that we should still be very careful. I was actually relieved when the u turn was made as the priority for Xmas this year is to do all we can to ensure we are still around to celebrate Xmas 2021.

28/12/20. Boris Johnson promised that the UK would not leave the Erasmus+ scheme. ✗His deal breaks this promise.

https://www.facebook.com/theSNP/videos/862277131203785

Broken promise? NO it's just another fucking lie.

Most people say I'm a clown. Yet they don't laugh at my jokes. Most people avoid me, because I'm a "clown". Yet I'm at the center of the circus. But I know I'm gonna be a clown forever. Because I can't take this damn mask off, no matter how hard I try.

29/12/20.

> **Lewis Goodall** ✓
> @lewis_goodall
>
> Replying to @lewis_goodall
>
> "Staff are near burn out with lots of them showing signs of PTSD. I see nurses and doctors crying on the corridors before, during and after shifts.
>
> To anyone who says this is not real they need to be shown the inside of a Covid ITU or acute admissions ward."
>
> 8:07 PM · Dec 29, 2020 · Twitter Web App

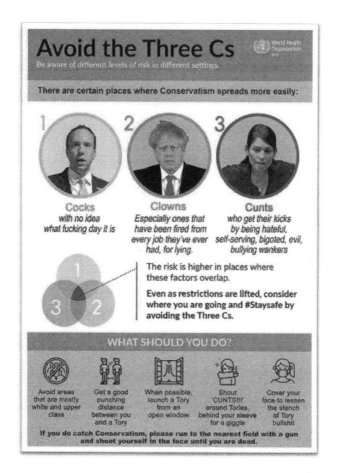

January: No need to be alarmed. It's a Chinese bug. We're bloody British. 🇨

February: It appears that the Italians can catch it too, but they rolled over to the Germans in the war so it's to be expected and not a concern for us. Stiff upper lip.

March: Errrr, it looks like we can catch it after all. However, there's no need to panic, just stay two meters apart and sing happy birthday whilst washing your hands. 👀

April: We could do with around 60% of you catching it, but you'll probably kill your gran in the process. This is becoming somewhat of a pickle we're in. 😬

May: Yeah, we've totally fucked it guys. It's spreading quicker than a 5g conspiracy. Stay the fuck away from everyone unless you fancy popping out for a McDonald's. 🍔🍟

June: You can definitely maybe get away with sitting within a meter of a perfect stranger in the park, but meeting up with a friend will lead to certain death so stay home, unless you want to go out.

July: You may get back in the pub, but only for essential drinks. Feel free to chat rubbish with a random person in the smoking area, but leave immediately if you see a member of your family, or face arrest.

August: Eat out to help out! Every single UK citizen simply must rush out to do all the things we've asked you not to do for the last few months. It's your duty, and here's a tenner on us for your efforts.

September: You ghastly, little cretins! Who told you to go out and spread the virus like that again? Have you listened to a bloody word we've said? Don't even come at me with your crocodile tiers, bro.

October: Work from home again unless your place of work has a till.

November: You can go and get your muff waxed and do a bit of Christmas shopping with thousands of others; however, attendance of restricted pubs, bars and restaurants still pose too much of a risk to mingle in.

December: Christmas is cancelled. See you all again in the new year for more absolute fuckery, you moronic arseholes.

30/12/20. After having dug to a depth of 10 feet last year, French scientists found traces of copper wire dating back 200 years and came to the conclusion that their ancestors already had a telephone network more than 150 years ago.

Not to be outdone by the French: in the weeks that followed, American archaeologists dug to a depth of 20 feet before finding traces of copper wire. Shortly afterwards, they published an article in the New York Times saying : "American archaeologists, having found traces of 250-year-old copper wire, have concluded that their ancestors already had an advanced high-tech communications network 50 years earlier than the French."

A few weeks later, 'The Archaeological Society of Scotland' reported the following: "After digging down to a depth of 33 feet in the Cumbernauld area of North Lanarkshire in 2011, Charlie Hardcastle, a self-taught local amateur archaeologist, reported that he had found absolutely bugger all. Charlie has therefore concluded that 250 years ago, Scotland had already gone wireless."

Just makes you bloody proud to be Scottish.

31/12/20 What Johnsons extreme Brexit really means.

Whether you are Pro SNP Indy supporter or a staunch Unionist- sit back watch and listen to the passionate, intelligent, eloquent and true statesman like speeches of Salmond, Black, Blackford and Sturgeon et al then watch the embarrassing, blundering, lying buffoon that is UK PM and tell me honestly who you think represents the character, sincerity, honesty and compassion of true proud Scottish people? By the way it is a rhetorical question unless you are an embarrassing, blundering, lying buffoon. 😎

https://www.facebook.com/watch/?v=897606977446326&notif_id=1609376698926562&notif_t=watch_follower_video&ref=notif

I have not included the replies or debates to any of my posts as I did not think it was fair to publish other people names and opinions and it would also have made War & Peace look like a quick five-minute read compared to how this book would have turned but I will make an exception as I start to wind up the book …..and some friends. LOL

• **Chris Thewlis**

It doesn't matter it's been passed. But what does matter is the fact that the SNP were prepared to vote if successful to place Scotland in a more difficult economic situation for their own political gain.

I cannot wait for Salmond to corroborate wee nippy Nikki's husbands evidence that she knowingly mislead a government enquiry by her own statement and the management of others.

She's not the first politician to have done this in history but I wonder if she will be the first to not resign after carrying out such actions?

Robin Hunter to

Chris Thewlis

yes, she probably will be the first not to resign.😎

Martin Hargrave

At least she'll be happy that there's a deal now and am sure that she'll get right behind the government now.

Tom King to

Chris Thewlis Jan Roman Rock Martin Hargrave Robin Hunter - I did say it was a rhetorical question therefore either your IQ is not high enough to understand rhetorical or you are confirming you are an embarrassing, blundering, lying buffoon. 💔Happy N...

Chris Thewlis to

Tom King

did you get a dictionary for Christmas 🎄 😄

Facebook created to allow people to voice there opinion and for others to then comment on that opinion?.
So rhetorically why would anyone post opinion like that from a political position of the denial of debate or response, surely this individual Tom King has chosen the wrong medium

Martin Hargrave

No!

Scott Miller

Going into 2021 I really do not know who the biggest slavering c@&t is ! I was thinking of many but after debate with myself and others we keep harking back to the same candidate ! But then again I'd suggest every single politician as well as Tom King are up for the award. C&@ts that like the sound of their own voice. 😊 Happy, Healthy & Prosperous New Year to you all.

Tom King to

Scott Miller

better late than never but thanks for confirming you are an embarrassing, blundering, lying buffoon therefore being called a slavering cunt by you is probably a compliment. 😒One of the many things that you, Chris Thewlis Jan Roman Rock and a few others that make comments that would be viewed as coming from individuals that know what they are talking about and who's opinions are by far the majority view and superior to slavering cunts like me is that in Scotland you are in a tiny minority that is getting smaller by the day...FACT Hamish Mair.......so who are really the slavering cunts? And that's not a rhetorician question therefore you are more than within your rights to confirm that you are indeed embarrassing, blundering, lying buffoons and slavering cunts. 😒😒 😒Happy New Year and Stay Home.....please.....you should not be allowed out in the first place. Luv n Peace 😊

Chris Thewlis to

Tom King

it was rhetorical and clearly stated it was rhetorical. Run along and read that dictionary you got for Christmas because you are using words you don't understand😒😒😒

Scott Miller to

Tom King

i your words Tom, stay safe, love & peace. May all you're windows be strawberry flavoured in 2021.

Martin Hargrave

Happy New Year, your political opinions won't make a toss of a difference also in 2021 and I hope everyone finds some inner peace and good health.

Hamish Mair to

Scott Miller

thanks for the glowing compliments lads I'm sure we will continue to rip the absolute pish out each other in 2021
Love and best wishes to you all for the coming year
Tom where the fuck are you going to perch when Nicoliar's tree comes down 😒😒😒

Tom King to

Scott Miller

maybe the windows should be fanny flavoured for the total cocks on here☺Love and Peace and I hope everyone has a safe 2021. 😎😍

Scott Miller to

Tom King

you'll struggle to get a window for your boaby !

Chris Thewlis to

Tom King

fanny flavoured would cleaning be free under the free prescription service????

Look forward to debating face to face in a pub each with a hand wrapped around a medicinal Tennants, come on 2021🍺

31/12/20. Close to 1,000 covid deaths yesterday, over 72,000 so far have lost their lives, the NHS is close to breaking point with worse to come. 99% of the UK is now in tiers 3 or 4 but Johnson says "we are not heading for a full lockdown"? WTF WHY NOT? Is Not Pritti Person Patel doing the math? Boris, I can assure you we are only at 99% we are a long way off 100%"

Gavin Williamson The "Education" Secretary....now there's a fucking oxymoron to end them all.....or just a fucking moron say's "We must get the schools open. Our children's education is important". Is education more important than lives? Plenty thick cunts get on in life without a decent education.....Politicians are proof.....but getting on in life if yer deed is way harder. What is wrong with on line tutoring and virtual classrooms? Has he already forgot to remember the spike when University students flooded back to crowded rooms and dorms?

Now back to 99% being a long way off 100% and Johnson adamant the UK is not heading for full lockdown. It's four months since his own scientists and the medical experts warned that full lockdown was the only way to avoid "catastrophic" death rates. Fucking Moronic Cunt.

Of course experts like Scott Miller, Roman Cock, Hamish Mair and Chris Thewlis will point out that Sturgeon is not much better as they have uncovered that she once got a parking ticket.....but claim she put it on expenses.

Now at the same time I rant on here New Zealand has just celebrated a restriction free New Year and have ZERO covid cases never mind a new strain. Why ? Two main reasons. First, their PM is obviously a shining example of how to tackle a crisis and took immediate action and imposed severe restrictions back at the start of the crisis and never wavered since. Secondly, at the start of the crisis the UK had Johnson and his boss Cummings deciding a cull of the sick, elderly and those on benefits was a sacrifice worth taking.

The UK is run by The Arseholes of The Apocalypse. Love n Peace n Stay Safe....to all those that deserve it. 😐 😎

https://www.facebook.com/NicolaSturgeonSNP/videos/672090333483480

Fare Well Part 1 - Edinburgh's Hogmanay 2020

https://www.youtube.com/watch?v=nV4jNWZlmEU

Fare Well Part 2 - Edinburgh's Hogmanay 2020

https://www.youtube.com/watch?v=5LKKmimrsx8

Fare Well Part 3 - Edinburgh's Hogmanay 2020

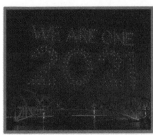

https://www.youtube.com/watch?v=JKUAZxqUorI

01/01/021. I am writing this at 00:01 am 1st January 2021 and I don't think I can be any clearer and passionate about my desire to see an Independent Scotland in 2021. However, the coronavirus crisis is far from over with the UK Government and Devolved Countries under pressure to make further restrictions to avoid a humanitarian catastrophe and the NHS being completely overwhelmed. Of course, it is a time of year we all wish to spend time with our loved ones and celebrate with family, friends and even strangers but the risks are very high of increasing the spread of infections. Families all over the world have missed once in a lifetime events such as important birthdays, weddings, births and unfortunately proper funerals for loved ones. No matter your religion …..please make sure we are all here to celebrate next year.

The only thing I can wish for more than Independence in 2021 is an end to the suffering this curse has brought to our world and that we can return to normality with the lessons and mistakes of 2020 leading us into to a Fairer Caring Society.

Love and Peace to All and Stay Safe. Tommy King.

Spirit of Scotland

In the year 2021
If God's a coming, He oughta make it by then
Maybe He'll look around Himself and say
Guess it's time for the judgment day
Tory rule has had its say
Now is time for Independence Day
It's been too many years
Scots have cried a billion tears
The sick and poor will have no fears.
Now the Tory reign disappears
In the twinkling of starlight
Scotland's future will be bright
In the year 2021
Scotland's Independence will be won
There will be freedom from Tory rule for everyone
Scotland's future will be bright and it's only just begun.
There will be a fairer caring Scotland for everyone.

By Tommy King

With thanks to Janey Godley for making us all laugh and allowing me to share her work.
https://janeygodley.com/

Created by Tommy King using original images available from www.wefail.art

Original images created by Tommy King
soon available at www.tickityboo.club   Contact tommy@tickityboo.club

In The Year 2021 – Full colour Flip Book.

https://designrr.page/?id=87376&token=768273918&type=FP

I more or less completed "Diary of A Lucky Bastard" between August 2019 and December 2019. Then our world was changed forever by Covid 19 and I put the book on hold. I hope this will be completed as soon as I feel life is back to non covid normality.

During lockdown I have published In The Year 2021 and I am now working on 2021 Vol Two. I also published "LOCKDOWN DIARY: MARCH 2020 - MARCH 2021 What a F**king Laugh ! and "Tramspotting ......for E.G.I.T.S.: Edinburgh Generating Integrated Traffic Systems. (EGITS). Spaces for Brains Emergency Edit".

https://www.amazon.co.uk/dp/B08QRVLSTX

LOCKDOWN DIARY: MARCH 2020 - MARCH 2021 What a F**king Laugh !

https://www.amazon.co.uk/dp/B092KN9TW9

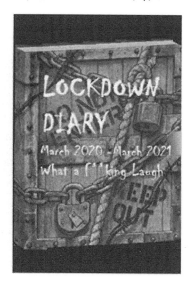

Tramspotting ......for E.G.I.T.S.: Edinburgh Generating Integrated Traffic Systems. (EGITS).

Spaces for Brains Emergency Edit. https://www.amazon.co.uk/dp/B094N3L2RR

Printed in Great Britain
by Amazon

66381948R00122